**TAXMANN®'S**

# MYSTERIOUS TEMPLES OF INDIA

Srinivasan Anand

© Taxmann

**Price :** ₹ 295

**Published by :**
Taxmann Publications (P.) Ltd.

**Sales & Marketing :**
59/32, New Rohtak Road, New Delhi-110 005 India
Phone : +91-11-45562222
**Website :** www.taxmann.com
**E-mail :** sales@taxmann.com

**Regd. Office :**
21/35, West Punjabi Bagh, New Delhi-110 026 India

**Printed at :**
Tan Prints (India) Pvt. Ltd.
44 Km. Mile Stone, National Highway, Rohtak Road
Village Rohad, Distt. Jhajjar (Haryana) India
**E-mail :** sales@tanprints.com

**Disclaimer**

The information provided in this book has been compiled from various online and offline sources whose accuracy and reliability is not guaranteed. Readers should take the information in the article only as information.

This book is published for general information purposes only. It is not intended to provide legal, business, financial, astrological or religious advice of any kind.

Adoption of any method, ritual, remedy or other information described in the book is entirely at the discretion of the reader. The author or publisher will not be liable for any direct, indirect, incidental or consequential effects arising from this.

The authors and publishers cannot be held liable for any errors, omissions or inadvertence. Readers should therefore consult experts or advisors in the relevant field as per need of their specific circumstances.

The purpose of this book is not to hurt any person, community or religious sentiments. Its sole purpose is to spread knowledge and information.

The content of the book is for your information only keeping in mind the public interest. Taxmann does not confirm the accuracy of the content.

# Contents

| Sl. No. | Temple | State | Page |
|---|---|---|---|
| 1. | **Where the deity drinks, half of the offering** | | |
| | ➥ Shri Panakala Lakshmi Narasimha Swamy, Mangalagiri Temple | Andhra Pradesh (Guntur) | 1 |
| 2. | **Where the stick ritual is performed** | | |
| | ➥ Devaragattu Mala Malleshwara Swamy Temple | Andhra Pradesh (Kurnool) | 3 |
| 3. | **Mysterious Water Temple** | | |
| | ➥ Mahanandi Temple | Andhra Pradesh (Kurnool) | 5 |
| 4. | **Where the Pillar Hangs in the Air** | | |
| | ➥ Veerabhadra Swamy Lepakshi Temple | Andhra Pradesh (Anantapur) | 7 |
| 5. | **Where from Statue Sweats** | | |
| | ➥ Tirupati Balaji | Andhra Pradesh (Chittoor) | 9 |
| 6. | **Where the Size of the Nandi Statue is Continuously Growing** | | |
| | ➥ Yaganti Uma Maheshwara Temple | Andhra Pradesh (Hyderabad) | 11 |
| 7. | **Temple of the Menstruating Goddess** | | |
| | ➥ Kamakhya Devi Temple | Assam (Guwahati) | 13 |

| Sl. No. | Temple | State | Page |
|---|---|---|---|
| 8. | **Where Animal Sacrifices are made Without Shedding their blood and without taking their lives** | | |
| | ➥ Maa Mundeshwari Bhavani Temple | Bihar (Kaimur) | 16 |
| 9. | **Where Idols Talk to Each Other at Night** | | |
| | ➥ Dakshineshwari Raj Rajeshwari Tripur Sundari Temple | Bihar (Buxar) | 19 |
| 10. | **Where the Size of the Shivling Increases Every Year** | | |
| | ➥ Bhooteshwar Nath/Bhakurra Mahadev Temple | Chhattisgarh (Gariaband) | 21 |
| 11. | **The Temple that Opens Only for 5 Hours a Year, with Thousands of Goat Sacrifices** | | |
| | ➥ Nirai (Nirai Mata) Temple | Chhattisgarh (Gariaband) | 22 |
| 12. | **Where Aghoris Worship the Goddess Even After Death** | | |
| | ➥ Kali Temple | Chhattisgarh (Raipur) | 25 |
| 13. | **Where the Waves of the Ocean Perform Daily Abhishek of Lord Shiva's Lingams** | | |
| | ➥ Nishkalank Mahadev Temple | Gujarat (Bhavnagar) | 27 |
| 14. | **Where Whale Bones are Worshipped** | | |
| | ➥ Matsya Mata Temple | Gujarat (Valsad) | 29 |
| 15. | **Temple Dedicated to the Sun God** | | |
| | ➥ Modhera Sun Temple | Gujarat (Mehsana) | 30 |
| 16. | **The Kalash at the Temple's Summit Weighs 10 Tons** | | |
| | ➥ Somnath Temple | Gujarat (Saurashtra) | 32 |

| Sl. No. | Temple | State | Page |
|---|---|---|---|
| 17. | The Temple that Disappears under water Twice a Day | | |
| | ➥ Shri Stambheshwar Mahadev Temple | Gujarat (Bharuch) | 35 |
| 18. | Where Zero Gravity is Found | | |
| | ➥ Tulsi Shyam Temple | Gujarat (Sasan Gir) | 37 |
| 19. | One of the Sacred Four Dham Temples | | |
| | ➥ Dwarka Nagri | Gujarat (Dwarka) | 39 |
| 20. | Where the Flame has been burning in cessantly for 1000s of years without any fuel | | |
| | ➥ Jwala Devi Mata Temple | Himachal Pradesh (Kangra) | 41 |
| 21. | Temple, Where Lightning Strikes the shiva lingam Every 12 Years | | |
| | ➥ Bijli Mahadev Temple | Himachal Pradesh (Kullu) | 43 |
| 22. | Mystical stone which is worshipped | | |
| | ➥ Kunzum Mata Mysterious Temple | Himachal Pradesh (Spiti) | 44 |
| 23. | The Idol of Goddess is Sitting under the Open Sky | | |
| | ➥ Shikari Devi Temple | Himachal Pradesh (Mandi) | 46 |
| 24. | Where the Headless Goddess is Worshipped | | |
| | ➥ Maa Chhinnamastika Temple | Jharkhand (Ranchi) | 48 |
| 25. | Where Criminals are Brought to Take An Oath | | |
| | ➥ Maa Mahamaya Temple | Jharkhand (Gumla) | 50 |

| Sl. No. | Temple | State | Page |
|---|---|---|---|
| 26. | Mysterious inscription behind the idol | | |
| | ➡ Maa Ugratara Bhagwati Temple | Jharkhand (Latehar) | 52 |
| 27. | A Temple where there is no Worship of Gods and Goddesses, Women are Forbidden to eat the Prasad and Prasad cannot be taken home | | |
| | ➡ Elephant Kheda Temple | Jharkhand (Singhbhum) | 55 |
| 28. | One of the Oldest and Largest Temples in India | | |
| | ➡ Virupaksha Temple | Karnataka (Hampi) | 57 |
| 29. | Sa Re Ga Ma Musical Pillars in the Temple | | |
| | ➡ Sa Re Ga Ma Pa Pillar | Karnataka (Hampi) | 59 |
| 30. | Where the Game of Fire is Played | | |
| | ➡ Shri Durga Parameshwari Temple | Karnataka (Mangalore) | 61 |
| 31. | The Temple that Opens Only for One Week a Year | | |
| | ➡ Hasanamba Temple | Karnataka (Bengaluru) | 63 |
| 32. | Where the Sun Performs Shiva's 'Abhishekam' with its rays on Makar Sankranti | | |
| | ➡ Gavi Gangadhareshwara Temple | Karnataka (Bengaluru) | 64 |
| 33. | Unsolved Mysteries of the Grand Murudeshwar Temple | | |
| | ➡ Murudeshwar Temple | Karnataka (Bhatkal) | 66 |

| Sl. No. | Temple | State | Page |
|---|---|---|---|
| 34. | **The Miraculous Shiva Lingam that Turns Ghee into Butter** | | |
| | ➥ Shivagange Temple | Karnataka (Tumkur) | 69 |
| 35. | **Sun's Rays Indicate the Month of the Year** | | |
| | ➥ Vidya Shankar Temple | Karnataka (Chikmagalur) | 71 |
| 36. | **The Mystery of the Temple Vault that Cannot be Opened** | | |
| | ➥ Sri Padmanabhaswamy Temple | Kerala (Thiruvananthapuram) | 73 |
| 37. | **Mysterious light 'Makaravilakku'** | | |
| | ➥ Sabarimala Temple | Kerala (Thiruvananthapuram) | 76 |
| 38. | **Where the Idol Gets Thinner Due to Hunger and temple remains closed only for 2 minutes every day to ensure regular bhog to Idol** | | |
| | ➥ Shree Krishna Temple | Kerala (Thiruvaarppu) | 78 |
| 39. | **Where Dogs are Considered Sacred and first offering of Prasad is to a dog** | | |
| | ➥ Parassini Shree Muthappan Temple | Kerala (Kannur) | 80 |
| 40. | **Miraculous Rahu Temple, Where Milk Changes Colour** | | |
| | ➥ Rahu Temple | Tamil Nadu (Thirunageshwaram) | 81 |
| 41. | **Temple built by stacking up stones without using any concrete or binding material and which appears to be suspended in air** | | |
| | ➥ Kakanmath Temple | Madhya Pradesh (Morena) | 83 |

| Sl. No. | Temple | State | Page |
|---|---|---|---|
| 42. | **Temple Where a Plate Filled with Liquor and placed near the deity's face becomes Empty in An Instant** | | |
| | ➥ Kal Bhairav Temple | Madhya Pradesh (Ujjain) | 85 |
| 43. | **A Temple that is an Unparalleled Example of Architecture and Design** | | |
| | ➥ Khajuraho Temples | Madhya Pradesh (Chhatarpur) | 87 |
| 44. | **Temple Where a Lamp is lit with Water not with oil** | | |
| | ➥ Gadiya ghat Mata Temple | Madhya Pradesh (Shajapur) | 90 |
| 45. | **Where Evidence of Ashwatthama's Arrival is Found** | | |
| | ➥ Asireshwar Shiv Temple | Madhya Pradesh (Burhanpur) | 92 |
| 46. | **The Temple Where the Soil is believed to be Miraculous and heals wounds caused by poisonous creatures** | | |
| | ➥ Maa Ratangarh Wali Temple | Madhya Pradesh (Ratangarh) | 94 |
| 47. | **The Temple with Tantra-Mantra** | | |
| | ➥ Chausath Yogini Temple | Madhya Pradesh (Morena) | 95 |
| 48. | **The Temple Where the Shiva Lingam Grows Annually** | | |
| | ➥ Matangeshwar Mahadev Temple | Madhya Pradesh (Khajuraho) | 97 |
| 49. | **Siddhivinayak temple - A Temple Dedicated to Lord Ganesha** | | |
| | ➥ Siddhivinayak Temple | Maharashtra (Mumbai) | 99 |

| Sl. No. | Temple | State | Page |
|---|---|---|---|
| 50. | **The Village Where Homes Don't have Main Doors** | | |
| | ➥ Shani Shingnapur Temple | Maharashtra (Ahmednagar) | 101 |
| 51. | **A Temple Carved from a Single Rock** | | |
| | ➥ Kailasa Temple | Maharashtra (Aurangabad) | 103 |
| 52. | **A Temple Built by the Pandavas in One Night** | | |
| | ➥ Ambreshwar Shiva Temple | Maharashtra (Ambernath) | 105 |
| 53. | **A Temple Representing the Movement of Time** | | |
| | ➥ Konark Sun Temple | Odisha (Puri) | 107 |
| 54. | **A Temple Where the Flag at the Top of the Main Spire Waves in the Opposite Direction of the Wind** | | |
| | ➥ Shri Jagannath Temple | Odisha (Puri) | 110 |
| 55. | **The Mysterious Temple Where it Feels Cold Even in Hot Summer Months** | | |
| | ➥ Kumhda Pahad Shiv-Parvati Temple | Odisha (Titlagarh) | 114 |
| 56. | **Where Just the Sight of the Deity Relieves All Sufferings of Devotees** | | |
| | ➥ Mehandipur Balaji Temple | Rajasthan (Dausa) | 116 |
| 57. | **The Temple Where Goddess Takes a Fire Bath** | | |
| | ➥ Idana Mata Temple | Rajasthan (Udaipur) | 119 |
| 58. | **The Temple of Rats** | | |
| | ➥ Karni Mata Temple | Rajasthan (Bikaner) | 121 |

| Sl. No. | Temple | State | Page |
|---|---|---|---|
| 59. | **Temple which could not be damaged by Pakistan's bombs in 1965 war** | | |
| | ➥ Tanot Mata Temple | Rajasthan (Jaisalmer) | 123 |
| 60. | **The Temple with an 80-Ton Heavy Stone on Its Summit** | | |
| | ➥ Brihadeeswara Temple (Rajarajeswara Temple) | Tamil Nadu (Thanjavur) | 125 |
| 61. | **Temple Where the Weight of the Idol Increases and Decreases on its own as it is taken out or brought back** | | |
| | ➥ Kal Garuda Temple | Tamil Nadu (Nachiar Koil) | 128 |
| 62. | **The temple carved out of a hill and sans any foundation - the Ellora of South India** | | |
| | ➥ Kalugumalai Vettuvan Temple | Tamil Nadu (Kovilpatti) | 130 |
| 63. | **The Temple Where Lord Shiva Came to Test Goddess Parvati** | | |
| | ➥ Ekambareswarar Temple | Tamil Nadu (Kanchipuram) | 132 |
| 64. | **The Temple with Musical Steps** | | |
| | ➥ Airavatesvara Temple | Tamil Nadu (Kumbakonam) | 134 |
| 65. | **The Temple with 33,000 Statues** | | |
| | ➥ Meenakshi Amman Temple | Tamil Nadu (Madurai) | 136 |
| 66. | **The Temple Where Bricks Float, and Music Comes from Pillars** | | |
| | ➥ Ramappa Temple | Telangana (Mulugu) | 138 |

| Sl. No. | Temple | State | Page |
|---|---|---|---|
| 67. | **The Temple Where Shadows Appear, but Not What They Seem** | | |
| | ➥ Chaya Someswara Swamy Temple | Telangana (Nalgonda) | 140 |
| 68. | **An Unconquered Mountain Peak that No One has Climbed Yet** | | |
| | ➥ Mount Kailash | Tibet (Mansarovar) | 141 |
| 69. | **Angkor Wat of Northeast India** | | |
| | ➥ Unakoti Hill Temple | Tripura (Agartala) | 143 |
| 70. | **The Only Vishwanath Temple in the World Where Shiva Resides with Shakti** | | |
| | ➥ Kashi Vishwanath Temple | Uttar Pradesh (Varanasi) | 145 |
| 71. | **Where the Temple Doors Close as soon as the Sunsets** | | |
| | ➥ Nidhivan Temple | Uttar Pradesh (Mathura) | 147 |
| 72. | **The Temple that Predicts the Monsoon Every Year** | | |
| | ➥ Varsha Temple (Jagannath Temple) | Uttar Pradesh (Kanpur) | 149 |
| 73. | **The Leaning Temple** | | |
| | ➥ Ratneshwar Mahadev Temple | Uttar Pradesh (Varanasi) | 151 |
| 74. | **Birthplace of Lord Kalki Avatar** | | |
| | ➥ Kalki Avatar Temple, Sambhal | Uttar Pradesh (Sambhal) | 153 |
| 75. | **Upon Entering the Temple, the Biggest Liars Speak the Truth** | | |
| | ➥ Narsingh Baba's Temple | Uttar Pradesh (Mau) | 155 |

| Sl. No. | Temple | State | Page |
|---|---|---|---|
| 76. | **Temple Where the Sound of Water Comes from the Steps** | | |
| | ➥ Ganga Temple | Uttar Pradesh (Hapur) | 157 |
| 77. | **Temple Where Footprints of God are Found** | | |
| | ➥ Rangmahal Temple | Uttar Pradesh (Mathura) | 159 |
| 78. | **Temple that Opens Only Once a Year** | | |
| | ➥ Latu Devta Temple | Uttarakhand (Chamoli) | 161 |
| 79. | **Lake of Skeletons** | | |
| | ➥ Roopkund Lake | Uttarakhand (Chamoli) | 163 |
| 80. | **The Temple that Remained intact depite being Buried in Snow for 400 Years and was Miraculously Protected by a huge rock from Devastating Floodwaters** | | |
| | ➥ Shri Kedarnath Dham Temple | Uttarakhand (Rudraprayag) | 165 |
| 81. | **The Land of Apsaras** | | |
| | ➥ Khait Parvat | Uttarakhand (Tehri) | 168 |
| 82. | **The Mysterious Temple, Where the Idol of the Goddess Changes Its Form Three Times a Day** | | |
| | ➥ Dhari Devi Temple | Uttarakhand (Srinagar) | 170 |
| 83. | **The Mysterious Temple, Where Corpses Come to Life in Front of the Shiva Lingam** | | |
| | ➥ Mahamundeshwar/Lakhamandal Shiva Temple | Uttarakhand (Dehradun) | 172 |

| Sl. No. | Temple | State | Page |
|---|---|---|---|
| 84. | The 1200-Year-Old Narsingh Dev Temple | | |
| | ➥ Narsingh Temple | Uttarakhand (Chamoli) | 174 |
| 85. | A Temple Where Chinese Priests Offer Prayers to Kali Mata and Chinese Food is Prasad | | |
| | ➥ Chinese Kali Temple | West Bengal (Kolkata) | 177 |
| 86. | Natural Cave Temples | | |
| | ➥ Gupteshwar Mahadev (Guptadham Cave Temple) | Bihar (Rohtas) | 178 |
| 87. | In the Lap of the Mountains Resides Goddess Durga Herself | | |
| | ➥ Shri Mata Vaishno Devi Temple | Jammu and Kashmir (Katra) | 181 |
| 88. | A Unique Example of Sculpture and Painting Art | | |
| | ➥ Ajanta Caves | Maharashtra (Aurangabad) | 184 |
| 89. | A Massive Temple Resting on a Single Pillar | | |
| | ➥ Kedareshwar Cave Temple | Maharashtra (Ahmednagar) | 186 |
| 90. | The Only Temple Where One Can See All Four Dhams Together | | |
| | ➥ Patal Bhuvaneshwar Cave Temple | Uttarakhand (Pithoragarh) | 187 |
| 91. | Cave Temples in India | | 189 |

# Mysterious temples of unbelievable India

The heavenly abode of the Almighty on Earth is referred to as 'Mandir' by the Hindus. You will find majestic temples at mostly every corner of the country. Every temple has a unique history and legend attached to it. During the ancient times, the Indian rulers would patronize artists and sculptures for creating exceptional masterpieces in the form of temples under their reign.

India is the land of 64 crore god and goddesses, with a multitude of holy cities and shrines of spiritual gurus to a motorcycle. Here, temples can be found at every step of the way, but only some of them are odd, strange, weird or unusual in one way or another. Some of these **mysterious temples of India** are famed because of their unconventional deities, some because of their exorcism rites, and some because they are more than 2000 years old. The mystery of the unusual temples of India will give you goosebumps. The country, known for housing 330 million temples (approx.), has some temples sure to shock you with their mysteries. Adding a dash of mythological significance, we present to you the extremely mysterious Hindu temples with spine-chilling and unsolved mysteries. If this sounds exciting, then lend us your ears!

From a fire that burns forever to a temple where evil spirts are exorcised, these places are for the people who have faith, or are simple curious. It houses several religions and places of worshipping deities. With the majority of Hindu people in the country, there are thousands of temples in India. With rich culture and traditions, people in India believe in stories that came from their ancestors. This can be experienced at certain places, particularly mysterious temples in India.

Labelling India as a 'country of temples' won't be wrong. It is the only destination in the entire world that believes in the existence of 33 million gods and goddesses. You can calculate yourself that even if there are two temples dedicated to each god, how many temples we must be surrounded by! All these temples come with their own history, legend and mythology, while some of these have interesting mysteries associated with them. You will come across various unconventional temples where deities mensurate, and some temples even have exorcism rights! The strange mysteries surrounding these temples is what makes them interesting.

They range in size from tiny structures located in the middle of roads to massive ancient temples carved out of rock. Some are famous and accented in gold, while others are much more modest. There are even some temples in India that are covered with erotic carvings. If you decide to visit a temple, please remember, no matter the size or condition, always make sure to remove your shoes before entering.

As there are thousands of temples in India, it meant a tough job to list down the most mysterious Hindu temples in India. However, we undertook rigorous research and have featured some of the most famous temples in India. Here, you would find a list of the **90 mysterious temples in India,** along with their magnificent photos.

So, let us engross ourselves in the wonderful journey of the mysterious temples in India. We are sure you would like to visit some of them shortly. These celestial places of worship are also major tourist destinations where devotees come in large numbers to worship Gods and Goddesses.

# Kedarnath to Rameswaram, Seven Shiva Temples in a line

**From Kedarnath to Rameswaram, there are 7 Shiva temples in a line along the longitude.**

There is a unique connection between Kedarnath Jyotirlinga of **Uttarakhand** and Rameshwaram Jyotirlinga of South India. Both the Jyotirlingas are present at **79 degrees** on the **longitude line**. There are also five such Shiva temples between these two Jyotirlingas which represent the five elements of the universe i.e. water, air, fire, sky and earth. The distance between Kedarnath and Rameshwaram is approximately **2,382 kilometers**.

It is believed that Arunachaleshwar, Thillai Nataraja, Jambukeshwar, Ekambeswarnath Temple of Tamil Nadu and Srikalahasti Shiva Temple of Andhra Pradesh represent the five elements of the universe. All these are situated at 79 degrees on the longitude line, which divides **India into two parts from north to south**. On one end of this line is Kedarnath in the north and Rameshwaram Jyotirlinga in the south. **Mahakaleshwar Jyotirlinga** situated in Ujjain of Madhya Pradesh is also counted in this line, but in reality Mahakaleshwar Temple is not situated at 79 degrees, but at 75.768 degrees. Due to this, it is slightly out of this line.

It is not a mere coincidence that these seven Shiv temples are in a row. These five Shivlings between two Jyotirlingas balance the universe. All these Shiv temples were established in different periods between 1500 and 2000 years ago, but the relation between the five elements and longitude between them is considered to be planned. These temples are in a row according to longitude, but the period of their establishment is different. Due to this, it is difficult to say that they must have been established with some special thought. But, whenever these temples were established, latitude and longitude were kept in mind. They have been established according to Vastu principles.

According to mythological references, Rameshwaram Jyotirlinga was established by Lord Rama in Treta Yuga before crossing the sea. On the other hand, Kedarnath is believed to have been established during the Mahabharata period, when after the Kurukshetra war, the Pandavas worshipped Lord

Shiva in the Himalayas of Uttar Path to please Lord Shiva. Similarly, these five temples have also been built between the 5th and 12th centuries.

## How are all the seven temples tied together?

Kedarnath of Uttarakhand, Arunachaleswarar, Thillai Nataraja, Jambukeshwara, Ekambeswarnatha of Tamil Nadu, Srikalahasti Shiva temple of Andhra Pradesh and finally Rameswaram temple are all built in a straight line. It is believed that Srikalahasti Shiva temple represents water, Ekambeswarnath temple represents fire, Arunachaleshwara temple represents air, Jambukeshwara temple represents earth and Thillai Nataraja temple represents sky. All these temples are built in a geographical straight line of 79 degree longitude. This line is also known as the **'Mystery of Shiv Shakti Rekha'**.

| Order | Temple | State | Element | Establishment | Longitude |
|---|---|---|---|---|---|
| 1 | Shri Kedarnath Jyotirling | Uttarakhand | – | | 79.0669° |
| 2 | Srikalahasti Temple | Chittoor, Andhra Pradesh | Air | 5th century | 79.7037° |
| 3 | Shri Ekambeswarnath Temple | Kanchi, Tamil Nadu | Earth | 7th century | 79.7036 ° |
| 4 | Shri Arunachaleswarar Temple | Thiruvannamalai, Tamil Nadu | Fire | 7th century | 79.0747° |
| 5 | Shri Jambukeshwar Temple | Thiruvanaikaval, Tamil Nadu | Water | 4th century | 78.7108° |
| 6 | Sri Thillai Nataraja Temple | Chidambaram, Tamil Nadu | Sky | 10th century | 79.6954° |
| 7 | Shri Rameswaram Temple | Ramalingam, Tamil Nadu | – | | 79.3129° |

## Let's know about these seven temples and their specialities.

In the middle of all these temples, India's special Mahakaleshwar Jyotirlinga which is located in Ujjain is present. The concept of calculation of time had existed in Ujjain even before the western countries. Ujjain was considered to be the **Central Meridian** of India. **Ujjain is considered to be in the middle in the relativity of earth and sky**. According to the time calculation, Ujjain has a different significance in the scriptures. On the basis of geographical calculation, ancient scholars have considered Ujjain to be on the **zero longitude**. It is also believed that the Tropic of **Cancer** also passes from here. Ujjain was known as Ozen in the Greek civilization. Ujjain was one of the most famous cities of the world at that time.

### 1. Kedarnath Dham, in Rudraprayag district of Uttarakhand

This temple is located at 79.0669 degrees longitude. Kedarnath temple is located in Rudraprayag district of Uttarakhand. It is called **Ardha Jyotirlinga**. It is complete by combining it with **Pashupatinath temple** of Nepal. It is said that this temple was built by the Pandavas during the **Mahabharata period** and then **Adi Shankaracharya got it re-established**.

The story of this Jyotirlinga is found from the **Devasura war** to the Pandavas. This is the only Jyotirlinga which is known as Ardha Jyotirlinga. Along with Pashupatinath temple of Nepal, it is recognized as Purna Jyotirlinga. The credit for re-establishing this Jyotirlinga located in Uttarakhand goes to Adiguru Shankaracharya. **The structure of this Jyotirlinga is like the hip of a bull.**

### 2. Srikalahasti Temple, Located in a place called Srikalahasti in Chittoor district of Andhra Pradesh

This is in Chittoor, Andhra Pradesh. Srikalahasti Temple, located 36 km from **Tirupati**, is considered to be the representative of water among the five elements. This temple is located at 79.6983 degrees E longitude. It is also known as **Rahu-Ketu area and Dakshin Kailasham**. This temple, established in the 5th century, was one of the main temples of the **Vijayanagar Empire**. **People come from far away to worship in this temple for Rahu Kaal and other defects related to Rahu-Ketu**. The peace of Rahu kaal is done in this temple worldwide.

### 3. Ekambareshwar Temple, Kanchipuram, Tamil Nadu

This temple is located at 79.42'00' E longitude. Here Lord Shiva is worshipped as the **earth element**. This huge Shiva temple was build by the **Pallava kings** and later improved by the Chola and Vijayanagara kings. In this temple, instead of water, **fragrant jasmine oil is offered**. There is a legend about the Ekambareshwarnath Temple in Kanchipuram, Tamil Nadu, that **Goddess Parvati performed penance here by establishing a Shivalinga from sand to please the angry Shiva**. This Shivalinga is considered to be the representative of the earth element among the five elements. Built in an area of about 25 acres, this temple is 11 storeys high. Its height is about 200 feet. This temple was established in the 7th century. The present temple was built by the **Chola kings** in the **9th century**.

### 4. Arunachaleshwar Temple (Annamalaiyar Temple), located on Arunachal Mountain in Tiruvannamalai, Tamil Nadu

This temple is located at 79.0677 E degrees longitude. It was built by the **Kings of Chola Dynasty** of the Tamil Empire. It is also called Annamalaiyar Temple. It is on the Arunachala Hill in Tiruvannamalai city of Tamil Nadu. The Shiva Linga established here is considered to be a symbol of fire element. Established in the 7th century, this temple was expanded by the

Chola kings in the 9th century. The height of the peak of this temple built on 10 hectares is **217 feet**. **Deepam festival** is celebrated here every year in **November-December**, which lasts for 10 days. During this time, a large number of lamps are lit around the temple. A huge lamp is lit on the hill of the temple which can be easily seen even from a distance of two-three km.

### 5. Jambukeshwar Temple (Jambukeshwarar Temple), Tiruchirappalli, Tamil Nadu

This temple is about 1800 years old. A stream of water always flows in its sanctum sanctorum. Jambukeshwar or Jambukeshwarar Temple is in Thiruvanaikaval (Trichy) district. This Shivlinga is considered to be the representative of water among the five elements because a natural stream of water always keeps flowing in the sanctum sanctorum of this temple. It is also mentioned in some mythological texts.

### 6. Thillai Nataraja Temple, Chidambaram, Tamil Nadu

This temple is located at 79.6935 E degrees longitude. It is built for the sky element. This temple is dedicated to Lord Shiva in the form of the great dancer Nataraja. The oldest depiction of 108 postures of dance is found in Chidambaram itself. The temple of Nataraja, a form of Lord Shiva, is in the Chidambaram city of Tamil Nadu. Earlier this place was also known as Thillai, hence this temple is also called Thillai Nataraja Temple. All the 108 forms of Natya Shastra told by Bharat Muni can be seen in this temple. Various postures of Bharatnatyam are engraved on the walls of the temple. The present temple was built by the Chola kings in the **10th century (Mystery of Shiv Shakti Rekha).**

### 7. Rameshwaram Jyotirlinga, Rameshwaram

It is believed that Shri Ram established Rameshwaram Jyotirlinga before attacking Lanka (**Mystery of Shiv Shakti Rekha**). It is one of the **12 Jyotirlingas**. The ancient temple of Ramnath Swami Lord Shiva is located on the seashore in Tamil Nadu, which is known as Rameshwaram. According to the story described in Ramayana, before crossing Lanka, when the monkey army was building a bridge on the sea, Lord Rama made a Shivlinga from sand here and worshipped it.

# Where the deity drinks, half of the offering

## Shri Panakala Lakshmi Narasimha Swamy, Mangalagiri Temple – Andhra Pradesh (Guntur)

The Lakshmi Narasimha Temple is a Vaishnavite temple located in Mangalagiri and one of the eight sacred places of Lord Vishnu in India. This place is one of the eight important Mahakshetras (sacred places) in India. In these eight places, Lord Vishnu himself manifested or emerged: (1) Srirangam (2) Srimushnam (3) Naimisham (4) Pushkaram (5) Salagamdri (6) Thothadri (Present Mangalagiri) (7) Narayanashramam (8) Vekatadri. It is also one of the eight Mahakshetras of Lord Narasimha in India. The temple is located at the base of the auspicious hill in Mangalagiri, which is part of the Vijayawada region in Guntur district of Andhra Pradesh. This temple is part of a series of three temples located on and around the hill; the other two are the Panakala Narasimha Temple on the hill and the Gandala Narasimha Temple at the top of the hill. It is one of the tallest gopurams in South India, and it is the only one of its kind in this part of India. The gopuram stands at a height of 153 feet (47 meters) and a width of 49 feet (15 meters), with eleven floors.

It is believed that one attains "Moksha" by a single visit to this temple. Lord Rama visited this temple for his mental and physical peace. After praying here, he regained what he had lost. According to legend, at Lord Rama's request, Anjaneya (Hanuman) permanently resides here as the protector of the region. Spiritual luminaries such as Shri Shankaracharya, Ramanuja, Chaitanya Prabhu, and King Shri Krishna Deva Raya have also visited this place.

In the temple, a drink made of jaggery and water (called "Paanakam") is offered as *Naivedya* as a regular practice. Devotees offer this drink when their wishes are fulfilled, and Lord Vishnu gladly accepts the Paanakam offering. The special feature of this offering is that the Lord accepts it wholeheartedly, and when the drink is placed in the deity's mouth, a strange rumbling sound is heard as if the deity drinks it to satisfaction. Half of the drink then flows out of the deity's mouth, which is distributed as Prasad. Another strange phenomenon here is the absence of flies or insects. Although jaggery, which is used to prepare Paanakam, is abundant in the sanctum, no one knows where the large amount of drink goes. The area always remains dry and warm.

# Where the stick ritual is performed

## Devaragattu Mala Malleshwara Swamy Temple – Andhra Pradesh (Kurnool)

The Devaragattu Mala Malleshwara Swamy Temple is located in the hills of Devaragattu village in the Kolagondu Mandal of Aluru constituency, Kurnool district. This temple is also known as the Gattu Malleshwara Swamy Temple and is considered one of the oldest temples. This temple is unique in our holy pilgrimage. Legends tell us that this temple is more than 12,000 years old. The Godhu Gattu hills are at height of 6,000 feet. Lord Malleshwara Swamy is said to be present here in the form of Kurma Avatar. According to the Gattu Mala Mallayya Purana, Swami resides here for the welfare of the people.

In Andhra Pradesh, there is a temple where devotees go fully prepared to either kill or be killed. Every night on Dussehra, the atmosphere in Devaragattu Temple, Kurnool district, becomes frenzied, as hundreds of people wield long sticks and strike each other on the head. It is similar to Dandiya, but with larger sticks.

At this temple near the Andhra-Karnataka border, a grand celebration known as the Banni Utsav attracts people from both States. The ritual takes place at midnight when the idols of the deities Mallamma (Parvati) and Malleshwara Swamy (Shiva) are brought to the Neraneki Hill temple.

Villages in Kurnool divide themselves into groups and participate in a ritualistic stick fight. After praying at the temple and performing "Kalyanam" (a ritual of blessing), devotees carry the idols down the hill in a cloth bag on their shoulders. Some devotees form a protective circle around the idols, and as they descend, rival groups of stick-bearers try to stop the procession, leading to a bloody conflict.

The stick fight continues at the base of the hill, with villagers—mostly farmers—covered in blood, walking in the procession. The procession continues until dawn, accompanied by various artistic performances by dancers, musicians, and singers, creating an extraordinary journey. Upon reaching the base of the hill, prayers are offered, and the temple priest offers a handful of blood from his thigh to the deity. Another fierce round of stick fighting follows, and the idol is placed on a throne, marking the end of the Banni Utsav.

# Mysterious Water Temple

## Mahanandi Temple – Andhra Pradesh (Kurnool)

**Mahanandi - The Temple of Mysterious Water**

Mahanandi Temple, also known as the Mahanandishwara Swamy Temple, is located in the Nallamalla Hills near Nandyal town in Kurnool district, Andhra Pradesh. The Mahanandishwara Swamy Temple lies at the base of the Shrishailam forest hills. This region of the Nallamala Hills contains nine Nandi temples: Mahanandi, Pratham Nandi, Nag Nandi, Som Nandi, Surya Nandi, Krishna Nandi (Vishnu Nandi), Vinayak Nandi, Shiva Nandi, and Garuda Nandi. All these Nandis are famous, but Mahanandi is the most renowned.

These 9 Nandi Temples are known as 'Nava Nandis'. The Mahanandishwara Swamy Temple is one of the 'Nav Nandis'. The temple is dedicated to Lord Shiva and not to the Nandi Bull which is his mocut (Vahana).

Ancient sages chose specific regions or pilgrimages as divine spots for meditation (tapas). A region or pilgrimage is considered sacred either by the presence of a deity (Murti) or by the flowing water (Tirth). However, this place is sacred and powerful because it holds both the Mahanandi deity and sacred water.

The water here has healing properties. During the winter season, the water becomes very warm, and in the summer, it cools down. The temple tanks' water is warm in the early morning and becomes cooler as the day progresses. Regardless of the season, the water here flows continuously. Temple inscriptions state that this flow has never stopped since the 6th century. Near the Mahanandi Temple, there is the world's largest man-made Nandi statue, measuring 15 feet by 27 feet. A unique feature of this temple is that devotees are allowed to touch the water near the Shiva Lingam. Devotees can pray and touch the Shiva Lingam, which is unusual since traditionally, the main deity in temples is kept out of reach of devotees. The newly added large pavilions in front of the temple provide good shade for the devotees.

Mahanandi Temple - Andhra Pradesh (Kurnool)

Veerbhadra Swami Lepakshi Temple - Andhra Pradesh (Anantapur)

# Where the Pillar Hangs in the Air

## Veerabhadra Swamy Lepakshi Temple – Andhra Pradesh (Anantapur)

The Lepakshi temple, located in Andhra Pradesh, is dedicated to the worship of Lord Shiva in his fierce form as Veerabhadra. It was built during the rule of Vijayanagara kings. The temple is noted for its intricate carvings, pretty colourful frescoes, and a huge 70 ft tall monolithic Nandi (bull) statue. The temple has 70 pillars, one of which is unique as it hangs in the air, making the temple special. Due to this hanging pillar, the temple is famously known as the Hanging Pillar Temple. It is believed that passing a piece of cloth beneath this pillar grants the fulfilment of wishes, that is why many devotees visit the temple.

The temple was built in the 16th century and is made of stone. It follows the Vijayanagara architectural style.

The Lepakshi temple is located in the Anantapur district of southern Andhra Pradesh, about 15 kilometers east of Hindupur and approximately 120 kilometers north of Bengaluru. The temple is situated on the peak of a hill shaped like a tortoise, which is why it is also called Kurma Sailabhi. The most interesting feature of this temple is a stone pillar, which is 27 feet long and 15 feet high, intricately carved. This pillar does not touch the ground, and hence it is also referred to as the Hanging Pillar.

There is also a self-manifested (Swayambhu) Shiva Lingam here, which is believed to represent the Rudra or Veerabhadra incarnation of Lord Shiva.

The Lepakshi temple is also known as the Hanging Pillar Temple. The entire temple is supported by 70 pillars, one of which does not touch the ground and hangs in the air. This pillar which does not touch the ground is known as the hanging pillar. The hanging pillar doesn't quite touch the ground and looks as if freely suspended in the air! There's a small visible gap between its base and the floor that gives the pillar an impression as if it's floating, defying all the rules of gravity. This pillar was once connected to the earth, but when a British engineer tried to understand how the temple was standing on the pillars, the pillar was disturbed, and since then, it has remained suspended in the air.

Often, a piece of paper or cloth is passed under it to demonstrate the mysterious nature of the pillar. This pillar has made Lepakshi popular among tourists.

There is also a footprint here, which is the subject of many beliefs. It is considered a witness to the Treta Yuga. Some believe that it is the footprint of Lord Rama, while others think it belongs to Goddess Sita. It is said that this is the place where Jatayu informed Rama about Ravana's whereabouts.

Devotees believe that passing a cloth beneath the hanging pillor increases wealth and prosperity. Additionally, the temple is linked to the Ramayana era. The presiding deity of the temple is Lord Veerabhadra, a fierce form of Lord Shiva created after the Daksha Yajna. Other forms of Shiva present here include Ardhanarishvara, the Kankala idol, Dakshinamurti, and Tripurantakeshvara, while the goddess is referred to as Bhadrakali.

# Where from Statue Sweats

## Tirupati Balaji – Andhra Pradesh (Chittoor)

The famous temple of Lord Venkateswara is located on the Tirumala Hill near Tirupati in Chittoor district of Andhra Pradesh. Here, Lord Vishnu is worshipped. It is known as Tirupati Balaji temple across the country and the world. According to Hindu beliefs, Lord Venkateswara resides in Tirumala with his wife Padmavati (Goddess Lakshmi).

> Lord Vishnu resided for a time at the edge of the Swami Pushkarini lake in Tirumala. You will be surprised to know that this lake still exists, and all the rituals of the temple are performed using the water from this lake.
>
> The idol of Balaji in the temple is made from a special stone. It is said that the idol of Balaji sweats, and droplets of sweat can be clearly seen on the statue. It is believed that no matter how many times the back of the idol is cleaned, it remains moist. Therefore, the temperature in the temple is kept low.
>
> It is believed that Goddess Lakshmi also resides in this form of the Lord. Hence, there is a tradition of dressing Balaji in both male and female attire. Every day, Balaji is adorned with a saree on top and a dhoti at the bottom.
>
> The hair of Lord Tirupati Balaji is real, and it never gets tangled and remains soft at all times. The mystery of how the hair remains real is unknown to anyone.

### Lord Balaji was beaten with a stick

To the right of the main entrance of the Tirupati Balaji temple, there is a stick. According to ancient beliefs, during his childhood, Lord Balaji was beaten with this very stick. The beating caused a wound on his chin, which is why sandalwood paste is applied to the chin of the idol.

When you put your ear to the statue of Lord Venkateswara, you can hear a sound like the waves of the ocean coming from inside. The source of this sound is still a mystery.

Inside the heart of Lord Venkateswara's idol, the shape of Goddess Lakshmi can be seen. Every Thursday, the idol of Balaji is bathed, and sandalwood paste is applied. When this paste is removed, the shape of Goddess Lakshmi appears in the heart of the idol.

A lamp always burns in the Balaji temple. The surprising thing is that oil or ghee is never added to this lamp. The mystery of who first lit the lamp and when it was lit remains unsolved.

A special green camphor called "Pachai" or Karpooram Pachha is applied to the idol of Balaji. It is said that if this camphor is applied to any stone, the stone will crack over time, but it has no effect on the statue of Tirupati Balaji.

Lord Balaji appears to be standing in the middle of the sanctum sanctorum, but from outside, it appears as if he is standing in the corner on the right side.

# Where the Size of the Nandi Statue is Continuously Growing

## Yaganti Uma Maheshwara Temple – Andhra Pradesh (Hyderabad)

This unique temple dedicated to Lord Shiva is located in Kurnool, Andhra Pradesh, about 300 kilometers from Hyderabad. The temple is known as Sri Yaganti Uma Maheshwara Temple. It is said that the temple was constructed in the 15th century by King Harihara Bukka Raya of the Sangama dynasty of the Vijayanagara Empire. The construction of the temple clearly reflects the Vaishnavite tradition. Additionally, the influences of the Vijayanagara, Chalukya, Chola, and Pallava rulers can also be seen in the temple.

According to beliefs, the temple was established by the sage Agastya. He initially wanted to build a temple dedicated to Lord Venkateswara at this location, but during the construction, the thumb of the idol broke. This made Sage Agastya very upset. Afterward, he meditated on Lord Shiva. Pleased by his devotion, Lord Shiva appeared and gave darshan to him and said that this place resembled Mount Kailash, and therefore it would be more appropriate to build a temple dedicated to him here.

> One peculiar feature of this temple is that crows are never seen around it. It is believed that when Sage Agastya was meditating, the crows disturbed him by constantly cawing. Angered by this, Sage Agastya cursed them, saying that they would never come to this place again, and if they did, they would die. Since then, crows have never been seen around the temple.

The biggest wonder of this temple is the idol of Nandi installed there. It is said that the size of this stone idol increases by one inch every 20 years. As a result, the pillars around the idol have to be removed one by one. According to tradition, at the end of the Kali Yuga, Nandi will wake up from his long sleep and appear in a giant form, which will signal the end of the world, where everyone will perish.

# Temple of the Menstruating Goddess

## Kamakhya Devi Temple – Assam (Guwahati)

Maa Kamakhya or Kameshwari (Goddess of Desire) temple is located in Guwahati, Assam, on the Nilachal Hill. It is dedicated to Goddess Sati and is one of the 51 Shakti Peethas. Goddess Kamakhya is also referred to as the "Bleeding Goddess." Apart from the main temple of Maa Kamakhya , the temple complex also has temples of the *Dasa Mahavidya* (ten incarnations of the deity) namely Kamakhya (Tripurasundari, along with Matangi and Kamala), Kali, Tara, Bhuvaneshwari, Bagalamukhi, Chinnamasta, Bhairavi and Dhumavati. Also, there are five temples of Lord Shiva namely Kameshwara, Siddheshwara, Amarakoteshwar and Kautilinga. The temple complex also houses 3 temples of Lord Vishnu: Kedara, Gadadhara and Pandunath. According to the belief, the *yoni* of Sati fell at this location on the hill. It is said that during the month of June (Ashadha), the goddess menstruates, and during this time, the temple remains closed for three days. It is also believed that the Brahmaputra River near the temple turns red during this period. The temple is also referred to as the "Yoni-Place."

The Kamakhya Temple is one of the oldest temples in India, with a history dating back centuries. It is believed to have been constructed between the 8th and 9th centuries. According to Indian history, the temple was destroyed once in the 16th century and was later rebuilt by King Nar Narayan Singh of Bihar in the 17th century.

Kamakhya Temple is considered the Mahapeeth of all the Shakti Peethas. Unlike many other temples, there is no idol or image of Goddess

Durga or Maa Ambe in this temple. Instead, there is a tank that is always covered with flowers. Water constantly flows from this tank.

> In Hinduism, it is generally believed that women cannot enter temples or perform any auspicious activities during menstruation. However, there is a temple in Assam where women are allowed to enter during menstruation. This temple is the Kamakhya Shakti Peetha, where the goddess is worshipped during menstruation. Moreover, a special prasad is given in this temple.
>
> The temple is filled with miracles, and the *yoni* of the goddess is worshipped here. Due to the presence of the *yoni*, the goddess is believed to menstruate here as well.
>
> In fact, during menstruation, a white cloth is placed in the goddess's court for three days, and after three days, when the court is opened, the cloth is found to be soaked in red, which is then given to the devotees as prasad. The cloth associated with Goddess Sati's menstruation is considered very sacred. This temple is one of the 51 Shakti Peethas, and Kamakhya Shakti Peetha is considered the best among them. The cloth is called "Ambubachi Cloth," and it is given to devotees as prasad.
>
> The Kamakhya Devi Temple is also famous for animal sacrifices, but only male animals are sacrificed here, not female animals.

After Kali and Tripura Sundari, Goddess Kamakhya is the most important deity for tantrics. The worship of Goddess Kamakhya is done in the form of Lord Shiva's new bride, who grants liberation and fulfills all desires.

In the temple complex, every devotee who comes with a wish got it fulfilled. In an adjoining temple, you will find an idol of the goddess.

The sacred abode of Goddess Kamakhya is known for tantra and mantra practices, and it is said that every wish is fulfilled at this siddhpeeth. That is why this temple is called Kamakhya. Sadhus and aghoris frequently visit this temple, and you will find tantric-related items in the temple premises, which are taken by tantrics for their rituals.

Near the Kamakhya Devi Temple, on the Nilachal Hill by the Brahmaputra River in Guwahati, there is the Umananda Bhairav Baba

Temple. It is said that the pilgrimage to Kamakhya Devi is considered incomplete until one visits Bhairav Baba.

In the temple complex, there is a flat stone shaped like is *yoni*, which is worshipped.

**Where Animal Sacrifices are made Without Shedding their blood and without taking their lives**

## Maa Mundeshwari Bhavani Temple – Bihar (Kaimur)

Maa Mundeshwari Dham, located in the Kaimur district of Bihar, is a temple associated with many mysteries. The surprising thing about this temple is that goat sacrifices are made here without shedding their blood and without killing them. Additionally, it is said that you cannot keep your gaze on the idol of the goddess for long. Inside the temple, there is also a five-faced Shiva Lingam, which changes color three times a day.

This temple is also referred to as a Shakti Peeth, and there are many beliefs surrounding it, highlighting its special religious significance. There are also many mysteries associated with this temple that remain unsolved. Here, goat sacrifices are made without bloodshed, and there is an ancient idol of Lord Shiva with five faces, which changes color three times a day.

On the hill, there are several stones and pillars that appear to have inscriptions of Shri Yantra and other sacred mantras. As you approach the main entrance of the temple, the atmosphere becomes devotional. Climbing the steps to the temple's entrance and reaching the top of the Pavra Hill, where the Maa Mundeshwari Bhavani temple is located, gives the temple a distinct spiritual aura. The ancient nature of the temple and the idol inside raises many questions about its history and the type of stone used in the idol's creation.

The temple is extremely ancient and deeply religious. According to legend, the establishment of the goddess at this temple is fascinating. It is said that in this region, two demons named Chanda and Munda were terrorizing people. When cries of people for help reached her, Maa Bhavani descended to the earth to destroy them. First, she killed Chanda, and after his death, Munda tried to hide on this very hill. However, Maa Bhavani reached the hill and killed Munda as well. This is how the place became known as Maa Mundeshwari's shrine.

Inside the temple, in the eastern section, the magnificent and ancient stone idol of Goddess Mundeshwari is the main attraction, where she is depicted in her Varahi form, seated on a buffalo. The idol is so magnificent that one cannot keep their gaze on it for long. The temple is built on four pillars, and its architectural design adds to its allure. The temple's connection to the Markandeya Purana adds to its mysticism.

> There are two particular mysteries inside the temple that no one has been able to explain, which draw people from far and wide. Even after witnessing these wonders with their own eyes, visitors are left puzzled about how they occur. According to the temple priest, the tradition of animal sacrifice has existed here since ancient times. Devotees offer sacrifices in the temple as a means to fulfill their wishes. However, the sacrifice here is different from those in other places.
>
> At this temple, the sacrifice of the goat happens at the feet of the goddess, but no blood is spilled. After the prayer, the goat is brought into the temple in front of the goddess, where the priest firmly holds its four legs, touches its head to the goddess's feet, and chants mantras. Then, rice prasad is sprinkled on the goat. As soon as the rice touches the goat, it becomes unconscious.
>
> The goat remains unconscious for a while, and when the priest recites more mantras and throws flowers from the goddess's feet onto the goat, the goat "wakes up," as if it had just been in a deep sleep. This is how the sacrifice process is completed, and this unique tradition of sacrifice has been followed for centuries. The goat is offered, but its life is not taken. This sacred tradition of animal sacrifice is one of the key features of the temple, which leads the devotees to believe it is a miraculous act of the goddess.

The miracles don't end here. Inside the temple, there is another phenomenon that will leave you amazed. In the inner sanctum of Maa Mundeshwari's temple, there is a five-faced Shiva Lingam, whose grandeur is unparalleled. Such an idol of Lord Shiva is very rare in India. This idol holds a hidden mystery that no one has fully understood or unraveled. According to the temple priest, it is believed that the color of the Shiva Lingam changes at different times of the day—morning, afternoon, and evening. The change in color happens so subtly that one doesn't even realize it.

# Where Idols Talk to Each Other at Night

## Dakshineshwari Raj Rajeshwari Tripur Sundari Temple – Bihar (Buxar)

**In a 400-year-old temple, statues perform miracles at midnight.**

In Buxar district of Bihar, there is a temple known as Raj Rajeshwari Tripur Sundari Temple, where the idols are believed to speak to each other in the dead of the night. It is believed that all the Shakti Peeths (sacred places of Goddess worship) across India are awake and sacred, and this temple is one of them.

This temple is 400 years old. The famous tantric Bhavani Mishra established this temple around 400 years ago, and since then, the priesthood has passed down within his family. The life of the goddess in this temple was consecrated through tantric practices.

Tantrics have unwavering faith in this temple. It is said that even when no one is present, various sounds can be heard from the temple. The most unique belief surrounding Raj Rajeshwari Tripur Sundari Temple is that, in the dead of the night, voices emanate from the idols in the temple. When people pass by the temple in the middle of the night, they report hearing voices.

This temple houses idols of the ten Mahavidyas: Kali, Tripur Bhairavi, Dhumavati, Tara, Chhinnamasta, Shodashi, Matangi, Kamala, Ugratara, and Bhuvaneshwari. In addition, idols of Baglamukhi Mata, Dattatreya Bhairav, Batuk Bhairav,

Annapurna Bhairav, Kal Bhairav and Matangi Bhairav are also installed here. It is said that strange sounds can be heard from the idols in the temple, these sounds resemble the voices of humans.

# Where the Size of the Shivling Increases Every Year

## Bhooteshwar Nath/Bhakurra Mahadev Temple – Chhattisgarh (Gariaband)

Located 3 kilometers away from Maroda village in Gariaband, this temple is situated amidst dense forests and hills. Surrounded by scenic forests and hills, it is home to the world's largest natural Shivling, known as Bhooteshwar Nath or Bhakurra Mahadev in Chhattisgarh. This Shivling is recognized as an Ardhanarishwar Shivling.

> Standing at 80 feet tall with a circumference of 290 feet, this is the largest natural Shivling in the world. The worship of this Shivling began when it was only 3 feet tall, and over time, its size gradually increased. The size of the Shivling has been measured multiple times, and each time, it has been found to be larger than before.
>
> Unlike other Shivlings which shrink over time, this Shivling grows in size each year, naturally expanding. Every year, on Maha Shivaratri and Sawan Mondays, thousands of devotees (*Kanwariyas*) visit this temple.

> # The Temple that Opens Only for 5 Hours a Year, with Thousands of Goat Sacrifices

## Nirai (Nirai Mata) Temple – Chhattisgarh (Gariaband)

Temples dedicated to various deities are located in every corner of India. Each temple has its own mystery, which makes it world-renowned. This chapter deals with one such temple that is unique in itself and famous worldwide.

This temple is Nirai Mata Temple. It is situated on a hill, 12 kilometers away from the Gariaband district headquarters in Chhattisgarh. The temple is located in Nirai village, which is part of the Sodhul panchayat, near the banks of the Pari River. It is a major attraction for devotees and visitors.

The temple is the main center of faith for the local devotees of the goddess. In Nirai Mata Temple, offerings like *sindoor*, *suhaag*, *shringar*, *kumkum*, *gulal*, and *bandan* are not made. Instead, coconuts and incense sticks are used to worship the goddess. Unlike other temples in the country where devotees can visit throughout the day, Nirai Mata Temple is open only for a limited time during the year: from 4 AM to 9 AM, i.e., for just 5 hours each day during Chaitra Navaratri. Thousands of devotees visit the temple every year during this short time frame to offer their prayers.

### The Self-Illuminating Light of Nirai Mata Temple

A special feature of Nirai Mata Temple is the self-illuminating light that appears every year during Chaitra Navratri on the hills where the temple is located. How this light is produced remains a mystery. It is believed by locals that the light is a miracle of Nirai Mata. This light continues to burn without oil for the entire nine days of Chaitra Navratri.

## The Temple Opens Only Once a Year for 5 Hours

The Nirai Mata Temple opens only once a year, specifically during Chaitra Navratri, and only for 5 hours.

The temple remains open from 4 AM to 9 AM, allowing devotees to pay their respects. After the priest conducts the rituals, the temple doors are closed for the rest of the year, and no visitors are allowed.

## Jatra Celebration during Chaitra Navratri

Every year, on the first Sunday of Chaitra Navratri, a Jatra (festival) is organized, and devotees participate in it enthusiastically. It is only on this day that the temple opens its doors for the general public.

It is believed that the Darshan (sight) of Nirai Mata should be done with a pure heart. Anyone who tries to enter the temple after consuming meat or alcohol is said to become the target of bees' wrath.

## How Mata is Pleased

In the Nirai Mata Temple, offerings such as *sindoor, suhaag, shringar, kumkum, gulal* are not made. Instead, the goddess is worshiped with coconuts and incense sticks. By this simple worship, Nirai Mata becomes pleased with the devotees.

The goddess, happy with the devotion of her followers, removes their fears and all their sufferings. When a devotee's wishes are fulfilled by the goddess's grace, they come in large numbers to offer prayers and worship.

## Thousands of Goats are Sacrificed

At Nirai Mata Temple, where it is open for only one day each year, goats are sacrificed.

It is believed that by offering sacrifices, Maa Nirai becomes pleased and fulfills all the wishes of the devotees. Therefore, people who visit the temple offer thousands of goats as a sacrifice to please the goddess. Some devotees also offer sacrifices after their wishes have been fulfilled.

**Unwavering Faith in the Goddess**

The people living on the hill, where Nirai Mata resides, have immense faith and devotion. Women are not allowed to enter the temple or participate in worship rituals. Only men perform the worship rituals here. Additionally, it is forbidden for women to eat the prasadam (offering). If they do, something unfortunate is believed to happen.

# Where Aghoris Worship the Goddess Even After Death

## Kali Temple - Chhattisgarh (Raipur)

This temple in Chhattisgarh is filled with mysteries, with the unique belief that Aghoris continue to serve the goddess even after death! The temple is famous for the belief that the Kali here is awakening.

Inside the cremation ground, there are several temples dedicated to Baba Bhairav. It is believed that this temple is the Jagrut Kali Temple (the temple of the awakened goddess Kali). With commencement of Durga Puja, worship rituals in many famous temples also started.

This chapter deals with a famous temple in Chhattisgarh, filled with mysteries. The mysteries associated with this temple are still being explored. In fact, the mysterious temple in Raipur, Chhattisgarh, is connected with many secrets. The locals believe that the goddess here is awakened. Many miraculous incidents have occurred at this temple, and even today, Aghoris serve the goddess.

### Maha Kali is considered the Goddess of the Cremation Ground

According to religious beliefs, Maha Kali is regarded as the Goddess of the cremation ground. Therefore, her worship is not performed in the usual manner. Her worship is mostly done by tantriks and Aghoris. In Raipur's Rajendra Nagar, there is a temple located next to a cremation ground. Inside the cremation ground, there are several temples dedicated to Baba Bhairav.

People believe that these temples are Jagrut Kali Temples (temples of the awakened Kali).

## This Temple is a Jagrut Kali Temple

Within the temple premises, there are small temples dedicated to Hanuman, Shani and Shiva. The Kali here is believed to be the awakened Kali. For nearly 60 years, a skull has been kept inside a glass box in front of the temple, and a continuous flame burns atop it. It is said that Aghoris, even after death, continue to serve the goddess in this temple.

## Many Other Mysteries

The temple is maintained by the temple priests and the devotees who work there. Devotees often gather to witness and worship. The skull in the temple belongs to Aghori Maharaj Asha Giri, who devoted his entire life to the worship of Maa Kali. According to the temple priest, Baba Asha Giri Maharaj was the head of the temple and served the temple for nearly 15 years. His final wish was that after his death, his skull should be removed and a light should be lit on it in honor of the goddess.

Several other mysteries are also associated with this temple. It is believed that those who are unable to have children, if they offer prayers at this temple and make a vow, their wishes are granted.

As a result, this temple is considered a famous place of worship. People also offer jelebi (a sweet dish) and bada to Baba Bhairav and seek blessings.

# Where the Waves of the Ocean Perform Daily Abhishek of Lord Shiva's Lingams

## Nishkalank Mahadev Temple – Gujarat (Bhavnagar)

Nishkalank Mahadev Temple is a Hindu temple located in Kolyak, near Bhavnagar, Gujarat. Situated on the Kolyak beach, it is one of the rare sea temples in India. The temple is located about one kilometer into the sea and is dedicated to Lord Shiva. The temple has five self-originated (Swayambhu) Shiva lingams, each with a statue of Nandi placed in front. The temple gets submerged during high tide and reappears in all its grandeur during low tide, promising to wash away the sins of its devotees. During high tide, the idol of Lord Shiva gets submerged, and all that can be seen from a distance is the flag and a pillar.

It is one of the few sea shore temples of India, located about a kilometer inside the Arabian Sea. Devotees have to walk through the water to reach the temple. The temple stands on a square platform and houses five self-originated Shiva lingams, each accompanied by a Nandi.

> During high tides, the temple gets submerged, and the Shiva lingams are hidden under water. At such times, only the temple's flag is visible. However, when the tide recedes, the temple emerges again. This temple, standing strong amidst the powerful waves of the sea for centuries, remains an unsolved mystery.

> The temple was specifically designed to withstand high tides, and modern engineers and technology experts have yet to unravel its mysteries.

A special fair, called *Bhadarvi*, is held during the Amavasya (new moon) of the Bhadrapada month. Although in full moon and new moon time, the temple is submerged during high tides, devotees wait patiently for the water to recede to offer their prayers.

# Where Whale Bones are Worshipped

## Matsya Mata Temple – Gujarat (Valsad)

It is well known that in temples, deities are worshipped, but in the Magod Dungri village of Valsad Tehsil, Gujarat, there is a unique temple where whale bones are worshipped. It is believed that about 300 years ago, a person named Prabhu Tandel from the village had a dream in which a goddess came to the seashore and collapsed there. Initially, Tandel thought it was just a normal dream, but when he went to the seashore with some people the next morning, they found a dead whale on the beach. After this, people considered it as the form of the goddess and decided to build a temple in the village. They installed the whale's bones in the temple and began worshipping them. Soon after, many villagers opposed the worship of the whale, and a terrible epidemic broke out in the village. In desperation, people went to the temple to seek help from Matsya Mata. Afterwards, the epidemic ended, and people began to believe in the goddess's miraculous powers. Even today, villagers visit the temple to pray for the prosperity and well-being of their families.

# Temple Dedicated to the Sun God

## Modhera Sun Temple – Gujarat (Mehsana)

The Sun Temple was constructed after 1026 during the reign of the Chalukya dynasty. The temple complex is designed in the Maru-Gurjara architectural style. Unlike many other tourist destinations in the country, this temple is generally not crowded with tourists, which only adds to its charm.

The Modhera Sun Temple is located in the Mehsana district of Gujarat. It is about 30 km from Patan and 100 km from Ahmedabad. Situated on the banks of the Pushpavati River, the temple is famous worldwide for its unique architecture.

Like many other temples across the country, the Modhera Sun Temple also fell victim to the invasions of Mahmud of Ghazni. Alauddin Khilji not only vandalized the temple but also looted the golden idol of Lord Sun from the sanctum and took the temple's wealth. It is said that Khilji desecrated the temple, causing it to be broken and ruined. After that, worship in the temple was prohibited, and despite the passing of centuries, no worship or rituals are performed there today.

> The temple was designed in such a way that, during each solstice, the first rays of the sun would fall upon a diamond placed on the head of the Sun God. This temple was dedicated to the solar deity, Surya. The Sabha Mandapa (assembly hall) stands on 52 pillars, which were designed to represent the 52 weeks of the year. On the temple walls, you can see carvings

depicting the unity of the Sun along with the four other elements – Air, Water, Earth, and Space.

At the base of the temple, there are countless elephant sculptures known as "Gaj Petika." One of the most remarkable features of the Modhera Sun Temple is that no lime or mortar was used to bind the bricks and stones together.

In front of the Sun Temple, on the steps, there is a temple dedicated to Lord Vishnu, sitting on the Sheshashayi (serpent bed). Around the sanctum is a circumambulatory path.

In front of the Sabha Mandapa, there is a large stepwell known as the "Suryakund" or "Ramkund." During Makar Sankranti, devotees gather in large numbers to have a glimpse of Lord Surya and take a holy dip in the kund. The sight of the temple's reflection in the water of the stepwell is truly mesmerizing.

> **The Kalash at the Temple's Summit Weighs 10 Tons**

## Somnath Temple – Gujarat (Saurashtra)

Somnath Temple is a significant Hindu temple and is considered the first among the 12 Jyotirlingas.

Located in the Veraval Port of the Saurashtra region in Gujarat, this temple is said to have been constructed by the Moon God (Chandra Dev) himself. It is even mentioned in the Rigveda. This place is considered one of the most mysterious and sacred. It was a major site for the Yaduvanshis. The temple has been destroyed 17 times over history and rebuilt each time.

Somnath Temple is situated at Prabhas Patan, near the Veraval Port on the western coast of Gujarat, in the Saurashtra region. It is considered the first of the 12 Jyotirlinga temples dedicated to Lord Shiva in India. The temple is a significant pilgrimage and tourist destination in Gujarat. In ancient times, this temple was repeatedly destroyed by foreign Muslim invaders and the Portuguese. After the repeated invasions, the current Hindu temple was rebuilt in the architectural style of the Chalukyas. The temple was looted by Mahmud of Ghazni, a well-known event in history. After this incident, the temple gained worldwide recognition.

According to Spiritual guru Sri Sri Ravi Shankar, some priests took away the fragments of a Shiva Linga from the famous Somnath temple in Gujarat after Mahmud of Ghazni invaded India in the 11th century and destroyed the Somnath Temple including the Shiva Lingam. In a clip shared on social media by Sri Sri Ravi Shankar's official handle, the spiritual leader said that after Mahmud of Ghazni attacked and destroyed the Somnath Temple along with the Jyotirlingam in 1026 CE, a few Agnihotri Brahmins secretly carried the pieces of the broken Shiva Lingam with them to Tamil Nadu, moulded them into small Shivalingas and continued to secretly worship them through the generations.

The social media post of Sri Sri Ravi Shankar ji says that "A thousand years ago, when Mahmud of Ghazni invaded India, he destroyed the Somnath temple on his 18th attack. Some priests then took the broken pieces of the Shiva Linga with them. One such family sculpted those pieces into a Shiva Linga and worshipped them across several generations. In 1924, the then Shankaracharya instructed the family to keep it hidden for 100 years, and continue to worship it. Now the Shankaracharya guided the family to bring it here to Bengaluru!"

These relics eventually came into the care of the family of Agnihotri Brahmin Pandit Sitaram Shastri who took them to Sri Sri Ravi Shankar ji on the advice of Kanchi Shankaracharya HH Vijayendra Saraswati ji.

As per media reports, Sri Sri Ravi Shankar ji has been entrusted the task of reinstallation of this Shiva Linga .

Originally, the temple was also known as Prabhas Kshetra, and it is believed to be the place where Lord Krishna gave up his mortal form.

It is said that the gates of the temple, now kept in Agra, were looted by Mahmud of Ghazni and taken away.

> "Somnath" means "Lord of the Moon" – referring to the fact that Chandra dev (Moon God) married the 27 daughters of Daksha Prajapati, but loved only Rohini. The other 26 wives complained to their father Daksha, who cursed Chandra Dev to lose his shine. Through the worship of Lord Shiva, Chandra Dev regained his shine.
>
> The Somnath Temple is dedicated to Lord Shiva and is located at a place where there is no land between it and Antarctica along a straight line through the sea.

The temple's spire rises to a height of 150 feet, and it contains a sanctum sanctorum (garbhagriha), an assembly hall (sabhamandapa), and a dance hall (natyamandapa).

In ancient times, the Shivling in the temple hung in mid-air, but it was destroyed by invaders. It is believed that 24 Shivlings were installed, with Somnath's Shivling placed in the center. Some of these Shivlings are located under the Tropic of Cancer in the sky.

The Shivling in Somnath Temple has radioactive properties that help it maintain balance above the ground. The construction of the temple took five years.

To the south of the temple, on the shore of the sea, stands a pillar called the Banasthambha. At the top of this pillar, an arrow is placed, symbolizing that there is no land between Somnath Temple and the South Pole.

Here, at the confluence of three rivers – Hiranya, Kapila and Saraswati – people come to bathe in this Triveni Sangam. The temple complex spreads over an area of 10 kilometers and contains 42 temples.

The Kalash (a sacred water vessel) at the summit of the temple weighs 10 tons, and its flag stands 27 feet tall.

# The Temple that Disappears under water Twice a Day

## Shri Stambheshwar Mahadev Temple – Gujarat (Bharuch)

There is a temple that submerges in water and emerges twice a day. This is the famous Stambheshwar Mahadev Temple, located near Vadodara, also known as the submerged Shiva temple. Situated a little away from the coastline, the temple becomes fully submerged during high tide, leaving only its peak visible. However, as the tide recedes, it reappears, and devotees can enter the temple to pray.

The Stambheshwar Mahadev Temple is one of the most unique temples dedicated to Lord Shiva in India. It is about 150 years old and is steeped in numerous legends. People often refer to it as the "disappearing temple" or "vanishing temple" because it hides itself from view twice a day! Why does this temple play hide-and-seek with its devotees?

To understand this, we need to know the temple's location. The Stambheshwar Mahadev Temple is situated in Kavi Kamboi, Gujarat, around 70 km from Vadodara. It stands just a few feet away from the Arabian Sea. Twice a day, during high tide, the temple becomes completely submerged. Recently, state authorities have built a spire on top of the temple, which is the only part visible during high tide. When the low tide arrives, devotees can visit the temple, offer prayers, and return. Flowers offered during low tide are carried away by the waves during high tide, creating a colorful sight along the coastline.

The transition from low tide to high tide is spectacular. It seems as if the water itself is offering its prayers to the four-foot-long Shivling found in the temple by performing 'abhishek' of the shivling.

> The temple, in the middle of the sea, appears thrilling even just in its visual appeal. Inside the temple, devotees can perform regular worship and rituals. However, the temple's most fascinating ritual is performed by the sea itself, morning and evening. When the sea waves rise fiercely in the morning and evening, it appears as though the waves are performing the Abhishekam of Mahadev. The peak of the temple is visible, but the Shivling is submerged in the waves. This divine play of Lord Shiva's "appearance" and "disappearance" has been going on for thousands of years.
>
> At this temple, Lord Shiva disappears for 6 hours a day. This remarkable sight occurs in the morning and again in the evening when the high tide arrives. Thus, Lord Shiva meditates under water daily for 12 hours. Devotees patiently wait with folded hands until Lord Shiva reappears.
>
> The temple is located about 85 km from the district headquarters, on the seashore of Jambusar, about 1 km inside the sea, and is accessed via a platform. The mystery of this temple lies in its sanctum, where the Shivling is visible only twice a day. Despite being submerged for centuries, the sanctum and Shivling remain unharmed. The Shivling is believed to be thousands of years old and was discovered in the same location where the Stambheshwar Temple stands today.
>
> Once the tide rises, the sanctum gets filled with about 1 foot of sea sand, which takes about 1 to 1.5 hours and thousands of liters of clean water to clear. The process of waves cleansing the sanctum is entirely natural. However, the biggest mystery remains: how was the Shivling installed in such a difficult location, and what technique was used to build the temple that has withstood the waves for thousands of years?

# Where Zero Gravity is Found

## Tulsi Shyam Temple – Gujarat (Sasan Gir)

The Tulsi Shyam Temple is dedicated to Lord Krishna and is situated in the heart of the Sasan Gir National Park, around 30 kilometers inside the jungle from Una. The temple is surrounded by hills, with the temple of Goddess Rukmini at the top. It is believed that when Lord Krishna and Rukmini had a fight, Rukmini, upset, ascended the hill, and since then, her temple has remained on the hilltop.

Tulsi Shyam Mandir is situated in Giri National Park so that during the journey, you can see natural beauty, waterfalls, river, mountain and also wild animals, lion, leopard, sambar, and peacock.

Tulsi Shyam Temple is famous not only for its religious significance but also for the unique phenomena that occur here, such as the Magnetic Hills and hot water springs.

> The Magnetic Hills area is located about 500 meters from the temple, where there is a zero-gravity zone. In this zone, a car will start climbing uphill on its own! Objects in this area are naturally pulled upwards, and water flows uphill.
>
> There are three hot water springs near the temple, with each having a different temperature. The sulphur-rich water in these springs is believed to cure skin diseases.
>
> 500 meters away from the temple is Bhimsa, a place where the five Pandavas are said to have stayed, and where Bhima is believed to have carved marks on a stone, which are still visible.

Many places from the Mahabharata era still bear testimony to the great history of that time. Some are associated with Lord Krishna, while others are witnesses to the penance and repentance of the Pandavas. After the destructive war of Mahabharata, the Pandavas continued their efforts to free themselves from the sin of killing their own relatives.

In the Himalayan region, there are many temples where the Pandavas meditated and prayed to Lord Shiva for repentance. One such place is located on the Arabian Sea coast in Gujarat, where Lord Shiva absolved the five Pandavas of their sins. This is why the Nilkanth Mahadev Temple was established here, where five self-manifested Shivlings (naturally occurring) are situated.

Maa Kamakhya Devi Temple - Assam (Guwahati)

Gupteshwar Mahadev (Gupt Dham Cave Temple) - Bihar (Rohtas)

# One of the Sacred Four Dham Temples

## Dwarka Nagri – Gujarat (Dwarka)

Located on the western edge of Gujarat, Dwarka is one of the four sacred dhams and one of the seven holy puris. It is the place where Lord Krishna is worshipped as Dwarkadhish.

According to puranic accounts, the city was originally named Kushasthali, where King Raivat performed a Yajna on the seashore. After the destruction of Kushasthali, Lord Krishna ordered Maya Asura and Vishwamitra to build a magnificent city, which was named Dwarka.

> Due to many gates (dwar), Dwarka is also called Dawrawati, Kushsthali, Anartak, Okha-mandal, Gomati Dwarika, Chakratirth, Antardweep, Vaaridung and Udathimadhya. There was a huge assembly hall in the city. The city was a hub for maritime trade, with over 700,000 palaces, gardens, and a large harbor.
>
> Dwarka has sunk under the sea six times and the current city is the seventh version, rebuilt near the old one.

**In Jain texts :** In Antkritdashang Dwarka is described as being 12 yojanas long and 9 yojanas wide, and it is said to have been built by the god Kubera, renowned for its beauty and wealth, resembling the city of Alka. Many Puranic authors believe that Krishna came to Dwarka with his 18 companions and his entire clan. He ruled there for 36 years. After his demise, the city of Dwarka submerged into the sea, and the Yadava clan was destroyed. It is also said that Gandhari, the wife of Dhritarashtra, and the sage Durvasa cursed the Yadu dynasty, which led to the destruction of Dwarka.

The current Dwarka city was established by Adi Shankaracharya. The Dwarkadhish Temple, the main attraction, was rebuilt in the 16th century after several previous temples were destroyed by the Mughals. The temple's sanctum houses a silver throne with a four-armed image of Lord Krishna, known here as Ranchoji. It is said that the place of this temple was previously a private palace and a Harigriha.

**Dwarka is home to two important sites :** Gomti Dwarka and Bet Dwarka. Gomti Dwarka is a holy site, while Bet Dwarka is a pilgrimage destination requiring a sea journey.

Archaeological excavations began in 1963, revealing artifacts over 3,000 years old, copper coins, and granite structures. Subsequently, the full city of Dwarka was unearthed.

# Where the Flame has been burning in cessantly for 1000s of years without any fuel

## Jwala Devi Mata Temple – Himachal Pradesh (Kangra)

The Jwala Devi Temple is located in Kangra district, Himachal Pradesh, and is one of the prominent Shakti Peeths. According to legend, the tongue of Goddess Sati fell at this spot, and that is why this temple was built here. The temple is known for a continuous flame that has been burning for hundreds of years, which amazes everyone. Devotees consider it a miracle, while scientists suggest that methane gas underground causes this eternal flame.

The temple is dedicated to the tongue of Goddess Sati, and it was constructed by King Bhuri Chand Katoch to mark this sacred site. The temple's construction was said to be aided by the Pandavas. However, the current structure was completed in the 19th century.

> What makes the Jwala Devi Temple so unique is that it doesn't house any idol. Instead, nine flames (representing the nine forms of the Goddess) continuously burn from the ground without any fuel. Among these, the largest flame represents Jwala Mata, and the other eight represent forms of the goddess such as Annapurna, Vindhyavasini, Chandi Devi, Mahalaxmi, Hinglaj, Saraswati, Ambika, and Anji.
>
> The temple is known as Jwala Mukhi or Jwala Devi, and it is situated about 30 km south of the Kangra Valley, and 56 km from Dharamshala.

> Despite several attempts to discover its origin, the source of the flame remains unknown. The continuous burning flame has never been extinguished and continues to mystify people even today.

# Temple, Where Lightning Strikes the shiva lingam Every 12 Years

## Bijli Mahadev Temple – Himachal Pradesh (Kullu)

There are many miraculous Shiva temples in India whose mysteries are yet unsolved. One such mysterious and unique temple is in Kullu, Himachal Pradesh, known as Bijli Mahadev.

It is said that every 12 years, lightning strikes the Shiva Lingam in the temple, breaking it into pieces. However, the local people do not suffer any harm from this. It is believed that just as Lord Shiva drank poison to protect living beings and became Neelkanth, in the same way, he absorbs the lightning for the protection of his devotees.

> The Bijli Mahadev Temple is situated at an altitude of approximately 2,460 meters in Kullu, Himachal Pradesh. The legend goes that once every 12 years, lightning strikes this temple, breaking the Shiva Lingam. This phenomenon has even been captured on camera, astonishing many. However, the reason behind why lightning strikes this temple remains a mystery. After the lightning strikes and breaks the Shiva Lingam, devotees still worship the same broken Lingam, which is reassembled by the priest using Makhan (butter) and reinstalled in the temple. Because of this, the local people sometimes refer to it as "Makhan Mahadev."

> **Mystical stone which is worshipped**

## Kunzum Mata Mysterious Temple – Himachal Pradesh (Spiti)

This is a divine miracle that continues to attract thousands of people from around the world, with a mystery that remains unsolved. The Kunzum Mata Temple is located at an altitude of approximately 14,900 feet in the Kunjum Pass, which connects the Spiti Valley to the Lahul and Kullu valleys.

The Kunzum La pass offers an incredible 360-degree view of the Bara-Shigri Glacier, which is the second longest glacier on earth, along with breathtaking views of the Chandra Bhaga Range and the Spiti Valley.

The Kunzum Mata Temple, dedicated to Goddess Durga (Kunzum Mata), is situated in a remote area of the Kunzum Pass. People traveling this route must circle the temple for protection during their journey. If they do not, they are believed to fall into trouble.

> Inside the temple, there is a mystical stone shaped like a closed fist. This stone is worshipped, and it is said that the stone reveals whether a person is virtuous or sinful. If you place a coin on it and it sticks, you are considered virtuous; if it falls, you are considered sinful.

> The interesting thing is that the coins used here are made of nickel, copper, and zinc, none of which are magnetic. So, how is it possible for the coins to stick? The scientific explanation for this remains unclear.

The temple is open only during a few months of the year, as the road is closed from November to March due to heavy snow. During this period, only local people are able to perform the worship.

# The Idol of Goddess is Sitting under the Open Sky

## Shikari Devi Temple – Himachal Pradesh (Mandi)

Himachal Pradesh, known as the land of gods and goddesses, is home to many historical and miraculous religious sites. One such remarkable site is the Shikari Devi Temple, located 18 kilometers from Janjheli in Mandi district, at an altitude of 3359 meters.

This temple, situated on the highest peak of Mandi district, is called the "Crown of Mandi." It is believed that the temple was built by the Pandavas. According to the legend, Sage Markandeya meditated at this spot for several years, and when pleased, Goddess Durga appeared and established herself there.

Later, the Pandavas, during their exile, also meditated here and were blessed by the goddess, who gave them victory in battle. They built a temple, but for some reason, the construction was left incomplete, and they left after installing a stone idol of the goddess.

> It is said that even during rain, storms, and snowfall, the idol of Shikari Mata remains under the open sky. Snow never settles on the idols of the goddess.

**The temple doors are closed, and the priest has also left the temple.**

At the start of every winter, the doors of this temple are closed. Due to adverse conditions during the winter, the priests also do not stay here. Recently, the SDM (Sub-Divisional Magistrate) of Mandi issued an order stating that no individual or trekker is allowed to visit the Shikari Mata temple until summer. This decision is taken in the interest of the public every year during the winter.

**Many people went missing and were never found.**

The Shikari Mata temple is situated on a high peak. Local people have reported that several individuals, disregarding the administration's orders, went to visit the Shikari Devi temple in the winter. Later, some of them went missing, and many lost their lives. Those who disappeared have never been found. Therefore, it is wise to follow the administration's guidelines. Going on this trek during the winter is essentially inviting death.

**The temple doors will open again in the summer.**

When winter sets in, the entire valley experiences heavy snowfall. No one visits here for nearly three months. After that, in April, the priest returns to the temple. He opens the temple doors and performs the worship of the goddess. Trekking is also only allowed during the summer.

# "Where the Headless Goddess is Worshipped"

## Maa Chhinnamastika Temple – Jharkhand (Ranchi)

The Chhinnamastika Devi Temple is located in Rajrappa, about 80 kilometers from the capital of Jharkhand, Ranchi. This temple is renowned as a Shakti Peeth. The Kamakhya Temple in Assam is considered as the largest Shakti Peeth in the world, while the Chhinnamastika Temple in Rajrappa is regarded as the second-largest Shakti Peeth.

Situated at the confluence of the Bhairavi-Bheda and Damodar rivers in Rajrappa, the Chhinnamastika Temple is also considered as a heritage of faith. The temple sees a constant flow of devotees throughout the year, but the number of pilgrims doubles during the Sharadiya and Chaitra Navratris. On the northern wall of the temple, there is a divine image of Maa Chhinnamastika facing south, etched on a rock.

In addition to the Chhinnamastika Temple, there are seven temples in the area, including the Mahakali Temple, Surya Temple, Das Mahavidya Temple, Baba Dham Temple, Bajrangbali Temple, Shankar Temple and the Virat Roop Temple. The beauty of the temple is enhanced by the confluence of the Bhairavi River from the south and the Damodar River from the west.

> In this temple, the worship is dedicated to a headless goddess. It is believed that Maa Chhinnamastika fulfills the wishes of all devotees who visit this temple, leaving no desires unfulfilled.

The great poet Kalidas described her in his exceptional words, "Puritaasesha Lokabhivancha Phale Shree Phale," meaning she grants all wishes in the wishlist of the devotees leaving no wish unfulfilled.

Inside the temple, there is an idol of Goddess Kali where she holds a sword in her right hand and her own severed head in her left. The idol has three eyes carved into the stone, and she stands on a lotus with her left leg extended forward. Beneath her feet, Kamdev and Rati are depicted in an intimate embrace, symbolizing the reversal of their usual positions.

Maa Chhinnamastika is adorned with a serpent necklace and a garland of skulls around her neck. Her hair is wild and open, and she is depicted in a divine form, nude and embellished with jewellery. Alongside her stand the Dakini and Shakini, who are drinking blood from vessels, as is the goddess herself. Three streams of blood flow from her neck.

According to legend, once Maa Bhavani went for a bath with her two companions at the Mandakini River. After bathing, her companions became desperately hungry, and their complexion turned dark due to hunger.

They requested food from the goddess, but Maa Bhavani asked them to wait patiently. However, the hunger became unbearable, and they began to suffer. To satisfy their hunger, Maa Bhavani cut off her own head with a sword.

Once the head was severed, it fell into her left hand, and three streams of blood began flowing from it. The goddess directed two of the streams toward her companions, and drank the remaining blood herself. Since that moment, the goddess in this form has been worshiped as Chhinnamastika, the headless goddess.

# " Where Criminals are Brought to Take An Oath "

## Maa Mahamaya Temple – Jharkhand (Gumla)

India is home to many unique and miraculous temples, each with its own set of mysteries. Among these are temples whose secrets have yet to be unraveled. One such temple is over 1,100 years old and is located in the Gumla district of Jharkhand. This fascinating temple, situated in the village of Hapamuni in the Ghaghara block, 26 kilometers from the district headquarters, was established in Vikram Samvat 965, more than a thousand years ago. This temple is a center of faith for Hindus, and its uniqueness lies in the fact that Maa Mahamaya is still kept in a chest.

The time when the Mahamaya Temple was established was a period of great upheaval. It is said that the area was haunted by spirits and ghosts. During this time, tantriks (practitioners of occult rituals) gathered here, and rituals and worship began. According to belief, criminals were brought to this temple to take an oath. Before entering the temple, the criminals would admit their crimes. At that time, the words of the temple priest were taken as sacred, and the people believed them without question.

On the new moon day of Chaitra Krishna Paksha (the dark fortnight), the Dol Jatra festival is celebrated here. On this day, the "Manjusha" (chest) is brought to the Dol Chabutra (platform), and the chief priest opens the chest to perform the worship of Maa Mahamaya. The priest performs the puja while blindfolded.

A belief associated with the miraculous Maa Mahamaya Temple is that the idol of the goddess cannot be seen with open eyes. As a result, the idol of Maa Mahamaya is kept inside a chest. Therefore, a symbolic idol of the goddess is placed in the temple, which the devotees worship. Every year, during the new moon day of Chaitra Krishna Paksha, the Dol Jatra festival is held here. During this time, the "Manjusha" (chest) is placed outside the temple on the platform, and after that, the chief priest performs the worship of the goddess. However, during the worship, the priest is blindfolded. The chief priest performs the rituals only on special occasions.

> **Mysterious inscription behind the idol**

## Maa Ugratara Bhagwati Temple – Jharkhand (Latehar)

India is a country filled with mysteries. There are thousands of secrets that remain unsolved till this day. One such mystery is the temple of Goddess Ugratara and the enigma carved on the four-armed idol of the goddess kept inside the temple. It is said that this idol is more than a thousand years old.

### Where is the Temple and Idol Located?

Between Balumath and the industrial town of Chandwa, on NH-99 along the Ranchi route, there is an ancient temple located at a place called Nagar, dedicated to Goddess Ugratara. This temple is a Shakti Peeth. It is believed that the temple is more than a thousand years old. The construction of this temple is associated with the ruler Pitambar Nath Shahi of the Tori State, and its renovation was carried out by Queen Ahilyabai. The beliefs associated with the temple's construction are mentioned in the Palamu Gazette of 1961.

### The Mystery of the Inscription Remains Unsolved

Around 25 kilometers from Balumath, near the village of Shri Samad in the Titiya or Tisia mountains, the Archaeological Department discovered a four-armed idol of the goddess. However, the inscription found behind the idol remains unread. This script is neither Brahmi, Devanagari, nor any other known Indian script. The script is completely different from all the known scripts in India, and what it is called remains an unsolved mystery for archaeologists and researchers.

## Beliefs Associated with the Temple and Idol

The belief is that the ruler of Tori, Pitambar Nath Shahi, while hunting, reached Mankeri village in Latehar. Feeling thirsty, he went to drink water from the nearby Joda Sarovar (lake). At the lake, he found two idols, one of Lakshmi and the other of Ugratara. These were the same two idols he had seen in a dream a few days earlier. After returning from the hunt, he decided to build a temple and had it constructed. Even today, the Joda Sarovar exists in Mankeri village in Latehar.

## Tradition of the Temple

The temple is associated with the Nath Sampradaya and is home to people holding the Giri title. The main feature of this temple is that it is free from any particular caste, lineage, or sectarian influence. The first priest of the temple was Panchanan Mishra, who was appointed by the king. The royal court-like system still exists at the temple today. In addition to the Mishra and Pathak families, there are other appointed roles: Purushottam Pahan who offers goat sacrifices, Ghansi who plays the Nagada (drum), and priests who perform sacrifices of Kaada during rituals.

The name of Queen Ahilyabai is also associated with the temple's construction. In this region, not everyone had equal rights to worship. During her visit to Bengal, Queen Ahilyabai toured the area and had the temple built to ensure that people of all castes had the right to worship equally.

There is also a belief that the tradition of the 16-day Navratri festival has been followed since ancient times. The festival begins on the morning of Matri Navami after the installation of the Kalash. Between the Saptami and Ashtami (7th and 8th days), there is a tradition of offering goat sacrifices, and on Vijayadashami (Dussehra), both goat and buffalo sacrifices are made. On Dussehra, a special ceremony is held where Pan (betel leaves) are offered to the goddess, and after the Pan falls, it is considered a sign that the goddess has given her permission for the idol's immersion.

## The Mysterious Region

To the southern and western corners of Maa Bhagwati Ugratara lies Chutubag, a mountain where the caves of Maa Bhramari Devi are located. In these caves, water constantly drips from several spots. It is said that about seventy feet below, there is a Satyugi banana tree, which, despite being centuries old, remains lush and green. It also bears fruit. Additionally, there is a stone with a hole from which water continuously flows, but this water is said to nourish only the banana tree.

## Who is Devi Ugratara?

During the Samudra Manthan (churning of the ocean), when Lord Shiva consumed the Halahal poison, to alleviate his physical agony, Adishakti (the Supreme Goddess) appeared in the form of Devi Tara and fed him her nectar-like milk from her breast. This act neutralized the harmful effects of the poison on Lord Shiva. Devi Tara is widely known for her three main forms: Ugratara, Neel Saraswati, and Ek Jata (the single braid).

Devi has other eight forms known as the 'Ashta Tara' group: Tara, Ugratara, Mahogra Tara, Vajra Tara, Neel Tara, Saraswati, Kameshwari, and Bhadrakali-Chamunda. She is considered a part of the Kali clan. Her direction is upwards, her vehicle is the jackal, her color is blue, and her nature is a mix of gentle, fierce, and tamasic qualities. Devi Tara is also included in the Dash Mahavidya (Ten Great Wisdoms) group.

The three main places associated with the Goddess are: primarily Tarapith in Rampurhat, Birbhum, West Bengal, Sughanda in Bangladesh, and Sasaram in Bihar, which are considered the major Shakti Peeths. However, in addition to these, there are also several mysterious temples and idols of the Goddess present in other locations.

# A Temple where there is no Worship of Gods and Goddesses, Women are Forbidden to eat the Prasad and Prasad cannot be taken home

## Elephant Kheda Temple - Jharkhand (Singhbhum)

Located about fifty kilometers from East Singhbhum district in Jharkhand, in the Bodam block, lies the **Elephant Kheda Temple**. In this temple, instead of worshipping gods and goddesses, the worship is dedicated to elephants.

The temple complex is home to numerous elephant idols. There is an interesting story behind this practice. In ancient times, this region witnessed a lot of elephant-related problems. Due to its proximity to the Dalma forest, elephants would frequently enter the fields and villages, destroying crops and causing havoc.

### The Story Behind the Name "Elephant Kheda"

To resolve the villagers' troubles, the priests began worshipping elephant idols made from clay. Over time, the elephant attacks started reducing. Eventually, a temple was built in the area and it was named **Elephant Kheda**, which means "to drive away elephants."

### Prohibition on Women Eating Prasad

As the temple gained fame, people from far and wide started visiting with their wishes and offerings. There is a tradition of tying chunri (a traditional cloth) and coconut, as well as offering sacrifices like goats. A unique custom here is that women are not allowed to eat the prasad offered at the temple. Additionally, taking the prasad home is also prohibited. The reason for this rule is not clearly known to anyone, though it has been passed down from ancestors.

The faith in the Elephant Kheda Temple runs deep among the locals. Many devotees come here to perform the Mundan ceremony (a traditional head-shaving ritual). According to the people, any wish made at this temple can only be fulfilled by simply offering a prayer at the temple.

# One of the Oldest and Largest Temples in India

## Virupaksha Temple – Karnataka (Hampi)

**This temple is dedicated to Lord Shiva and its story is related to Ravana.**

The Virupaksha Temple is located in Hampi, Karnataka. It is one of the famous temples in the region. The temple is situated in Bellary district, approximately 353 kilometers from Bangalore. There is also a belief that Hampi was the Kishkindha of the Ramayana era. In this temple, Lord Shiva is worshipped in his Virupaksha form. The story of this ancient temple is connected to Ravana, who was a great devotee of Lord Shiva. Located on the banks of the Tungabhadra River, the Shiva Lingam in this temple is tilted towards the south. According to legend, when Lord Shiva blessed Ravana with a divine Shiva Lingam, he also made a condition that wherever Ravana would place the Lingam, it would be established there. While Ravana was on his way to Lanka carrying the Shiva Lingam, he stopped to relieve himself and handed the Lingam to an old man. The old man placed the Lingam on the ground, and after that, Ravana was unable to move it. Eventually, a famous temple dedicated to Lord Shiva was established at that spot.

> One of the unique features of the temple is that mathematical concepts were used in its design and decoration. The temple exhibits repeated patterns that illustrate the concept of fractals. The main structure of the temple is triangular, and as you look

> at the temple's top, the patterns divide and repeat, much like you would see in a snowflake or other natural phenomena.

The temple is dedicated to Lord Virupaksha (a form of Shiva) and his consort Devi Pampa. Virupakh is considered to be a form of Shiva which is worshipped here. Construction of the temple began in the 7th century.

The Virupaksha Temple is located in Hampi, Bellary district, Karnataka, as part of a complex of monuments that have been designated as a UNESCO World Heritage Site. The temple is dedicated to Lord Virupaksha, a form of Lord Shiva. The temple was built under the reign of King Deva Raya II of the Vijayanagar Empire, by a commander named Lakkan Dandesha, also known as Proda Deva Raya.

Currently, the main temple consists of a garbhagriha (sanctum), three eastern chambers, a pillared hall, and an open pillared hall. The temple is adorned with intricately carved pillars. Surrounding the temple are a pillared cloister, an entrance gateway, a courtyard, small temples, and other structures.

The nine-tiered eastern entrance, the largest of its kind at 50 meters, is well-proportioned and includes some ancient structures. It has a brick superstructure and a stone base, leading to an outer courtyard with several sub-temples.

A smaller eastern entrance leads to the inner courtyard, which houses numerous small temples. To the north, there is another gateway known as the Kanakgiri Gopuram, which leads to a small enclosure with supporting temples, eventually reaching the Tungabhadra River.

A narrow channel of the Tungabhadra River flows alongside the temple's roof and descends into the temple kitchen before exiting through the outer courtyard.

# Sa Re Ga Ma Musical Pillars in the Temple

## Sa Re Ga Ma Pa Pillar – Karnataka (Hampi)

The Vitthala Temple in Hampi is world-famous for its 56 musical pillars, also known as the Sa Re Ga Ma pillars. These pillars are renowned for the melodious sounds they emit when struck. If someone gently taps the pillars, they can actually hear musical tunes. The mandapa of the temple consists of a group of main pillars and several smaller ones, with each pillar supporting the roof of the hall. While the main pillars are designed in the style of musical instruments, each main pillar is made up of seven smaller pillars that emit musical notes. The sounds produced by these pillars vary, depending on whether they are struck in a manner that imitates string, percussion, or wind instruments. When sandalwood is struck on the pillars, they produce rhythmic sounds that are close to the notes of Sa Re Ga Ma.

Hampi, a famous and popular tourist destination in Karnataka, was once part of the Vijayanagara Empire. There was a time when Hampi used to be very rich and luxurious. During the 14th century, King Devarav had a grand temple built here, called the Vitthala Temple, which is dedicated to Lord Vishnu. Later, during the reign of King Krishnadevaraya, the temple was expanded. This temple is considered the most beautiful among all the ancient temples and buildings in Hampi. The Vitthala Temple is also known as the Shri Vijay Vitthala Temple, where Lord Vishnu resides in his Vitthala form.

Hampi is not just a great tourist site; it is also a center of research for scholars from around the world. Therefore, this region has been designated as a UNESCO World Heritage Site. The architecture of this temple follows the Dravidian construction style. The temple is built from intricately carved stones, with beautifully sculpted figures and forms that display the finest craftsmanship, paying attention to even the smallest details.

This temple, while attracting tourists and devotees, also captivates researchers due to its uniquely constructed pillars. The temple has several mandapas–Sabha Mandapa, Ranga Mandapa, Kalyana Mandapa, and Utsava Mandapa–each of which is adorned with meticulous and enchanting sculptures, whether it is on the walls, ceilings, or even the columns.

Among these, the most astonishing feature is the 56 pillars present in the Ranga Mandapa, which actually produce musical notes. When any object strikes these pillars, they emit different kinds of sweet tunes. Researchers explain that each main pillar is surrounded by a set of smaller pillars, each set producing sounds similar to different musical instruments. It is said that this temple was built with the intelligence and craftsmanship of the best architects, sculptors, and other skilled artisans of that time.

> What is truly astonishing is that the tunes produced by these pillars could only be made with stones and mixtures of chemicals that were, as per modern science, only created in the 19th century in the Soviet Union. However, these sounds were being produced in India centuries ago. This presents a mystery to researchers, as there is no clear explanation for how such remarkable technology and knowledge existed in ancient India. This knowledge was preserved in written form in the Nalanda University centuries ago, and had it not been destroyed by fire, one can only imagine how advanced our country might have been today.

It is indeed true that our ancient ancestors possessed knowledge in fields that the people of other countries could not even have dreamed of at the time–be it in architecture, space science, or the intricacies of medical sciences. And this treasure of knowledge was stored at Nalanda University, a place of great learning, long before the modern era. If Nalanda had not been destroyed, we can only wonder where our country might have been today.

# Where the Game of Fire is Played

## Shri Durga Parameshwari Temple – Karnataka (Mangalore)

**A temple in India where people play with embers for eight days.**

Here is the unique story of this temple, which will leave you astonished. It is a temple of Goddess Durga in India where people play with embers for eight days.

This temple is called Durga Parameshwari Temple. It is located in the temple turn of kateel which is located about 30 km from Mangalore in Karnataka. The temple is dedicated to Goddess Durga and is also known as the Kateel Temple. During the festival of Navratri, a large number of devotees gather at this temple. It is said that during these nine days, the game of fire (*Agni Keli*) is played here. Let's find out why this game of fire is played here.

> Every year, during the Navratri festival in the month of April, the game of fire (*Agni Keli*) is played for 8 consecutive days beginning on the eve of the Mesha Sankramana Day. The game begins a day before the Mesh Sankranti. People come from far and wide to witness this event. For those who see it for the first time, it is an exhilarating sight. The tradition is called *Agni Keli* or *Thorthedhara*, and it

takes place between the villages of Athur and Kallattur. In this game, people throw firebrands (made from coconut husks) at each other. This game lasts for about 15 minutes. People believe that by participating in this game, their sorrows are reduced.

The Rules of *Agni Keli* game are as follows:

- The participant-devotees are divided into two groups facing one another from a distance of about 15 to 30 metres.
- The men wield burning palm fronds in their hands in order to hit as many contenders as possible in the other group.
- Each participant is permitted five throws, and this makes every throw count.
- Men wear cotton *lungi* to avoid catching fire, yet some of them do get burnt a little here and there. Therefore, first-aid is immediately given to the burnt participants in the form of *Kumkumarchana*, a type of holy water.
- Referees wearing white *dhotis* keep a watch on the fire throws. They control unfair play and personal attacks on any person.
- The entire fire play ritual lasts for 15 minutes or so.
- Once the fire fight is over, the devotees walk towards the Durga shrine where another short fire battle ensues lasting 5 minutes.
- Once over, the participants take the blessings of Durga Devi.

The entrance to this temple is called the *Gopura*, which is the first attraction of the temple. It stands about 108 feet tall and captures the attention of anyone who sees it. Once inside the temple, you can witness all nine different avatars of Goddess Durga in one place.

# The Temple that Opens Only for One Week a Year

## Hasanamba Temple – Karnataka (Bengaluru)

Among the many mysterious temples of India, one name that stands out is the **Hasanamba Temple**. This temple is dedicated to **Goddess Amba**, who is regarded as the presiding deity of Hassan. The term 'Hasanamba' means the **Smiling Goddess/Mother**.

The temple is located in **Hassan**, a place 180 kilometers away from **Bengaluru**, the capital of Karnataka. This area was previously known as **Sinmhasanapura**. The temple was built in the **12th century CE**.

> The temple is filled with mysteries. The most intriguing fact about this temple is that it opens only once a year – and that too only on **Diwali**. During Diwali, the temple is opened for a **week** for worship and rituals. After the prayers, the temple doors are closed again, and they remain sealed for the entire year. The doors are reopened only the following year.
>
> What makes this even more fascinating is that before the temple doors are closed, devotees come to offer prayers, light **ghee lamps**, and place **flowers** and **cooked rice** as offerings. After the doors are shut, the **lamp continues to burn** and the offerings remain **fresh**, even when the temple doors are opened a year later.

> **Where the Sun Performs Shiva's 'Abhishekam' with its rays on Makar Sankranti**

### Gavi Gangadhareshwara Temple – Karnataka (Bengaluru)

The **Gavi Gangadhareshwara Temple** was constructed by **Kempe Gowda** in the 9th century and later renovated in the 16th century. One of the temple's unique features is that the **Shivalinga** present there is **self-manifested**–meaning it was not made by anyone, but appeared on its own. According to belief, this **Shivalinga** spontaneously manifested.

Every year on **Makar Sankranti**, an extraordinary event takes place in this temple. On this day, the Sun God performs an **abhishekam** (ritual bathing) of the Shivalinga with his rays. The architectural design of the temple is quite unique. It is oriented towards the southwest, i.e., the **Nayrittya** direction, and it is built in such a way that only once a year do the Sun's rays reach the Shivalinga. This suggests that the temple's architect was knowledgeable in **astronomy** and celestial science.

> What is most astonishing about this temple is that, throughout the year, the Sun's rays do not fall on the Shivalinga except on **Makar Sankranti**. On this day, when the Sun moves into the **Uttarayana** phase, its rays touch the Shivalinga for about 5 to 8 minutes, illuminating the sanctum sanctorum. This spectacle is truly magnificent, and a large crowd of devotees gathers to witness it.

A secret tunnel connects this temple to the shivganga Temple which is 50 kms away where ghee poured on Shivalingam turas into butter. [*See* Chapter 34]

# Unsolved Mysteries of the Grand Murudeshwar Temple

## Murudeshwar Temple – Karnataka (Bhatkal)

Situated in the coastal region of Karnataka, **Murudeshwar** is a sacred site that has attracted pilgrims and travelers for centuries. However, this temple is not only famous for its magnificent beauty and spiritual significance but also for its many mysteries, making it a timeless location.

### 1. The Incomplete Tower – Why Was It Left Incomplete?

The **Gopuram** of the **Murudeshwar Temple** is a testament to human devotion and divine inspiration. At a height of **20 floors**, it dominates the horizon, leaving everyone who sees it in awe. However, there is a mystery hidden in its grandeur that has perplexed visitors and historians for centuries–the **eastern part** of the tower is **incomplete**. Why was such a magnificent structure left unfinished, after so many years of hard work?

### 2. The Mysterious Lingam – Immovable Even by Gods

In the ancient age of gods and demons, a powerful demon king named **Ravana**, known for his immense strength and devotion to Lord Shiva, sought the **Atma Lingam**, a sacred relic believed to hold the soul of Lord Shiva. Whoever possessed it would be granted invincibility. After years of severe penance, Lord Shiva was pleased with Ravana and agreed to give him the **Atma Lingam**, but with one condition: it must never touch the ground. If it did, it would root itself there permanently and could never be moved again.

The Atma Lingam settled in Murudeshwar, radiating divine energy. Even today, it is believed to protect the area and its people with its sacred vibrations. For devotees, the immovable lingam is more than just a relic–it is a profound reminder of the limits of power and the supremacy of divine will. Standing before it invokes a sense of humility, inspiring us to surrender our ego and trust the greater cosmic order.

### 3. The Giant Shiva Statue – Eyes That Appear Alive

Standing 123 feet tall against the backdrop of the blue Arabian Sea, the Shiva statue at Murudeshwar is not merely a monument–it is an experience. As you approach this colossal wonder, a powerful sensation overcomes you, as though the calm but potent gaze of Lord Shiva is watching over you. The closer you get, the more intense this feeling becomes, making it seem as though it is not a statue, but a living presence, silently observing and connecting with every soul. Many devotees recall this experience–no matter where they stand, it feels as though Shiva's eyes are following them, exuding a quiet but commanding energy. For some, this gaze brings peace and comfort, while for others, it evokes awe and reverence. The feeling of being "watched" by God has moved many to tears, as though their innermost struggles and joys are laid bare before a higher power. For believers, Shiva's eyes symbolize his omnipresence and omniscience, reminding us that no matter where we are or what we face, his gaze is always upon us, offering guidance, protection, and grace.

### 4. The Underwater Temple – A Hidden Temple Beneath the Waves

The beauty of Murudeshwar is not just above the ground; its mysteries extend beneath the waves of the Arabian Sea. Local fishermen and residents speak of an ancient submerged temple near the temple complex–an area that has been lost to time but not to memory. Stories of this submerged temple are whispered in reverence, sparking curiosity and awe among pilgrims and travelers.

It is said that on some quiet nights, fishermen have seen a golden light shining from beneath the water. Others have heard the faint sound of temple bells carried on the sea breeze. These beautiful moments have only strengthened the belief that a sacred temple lies quietly beneath the waves, untouched by time.

## 5. The Eternal Flame That Never Extinguishes

Within the sanctum of Murudeshwar Temple, there is a simple but extraordinary sight: a small oil lamp that has been burning continuously for centuries. On the surface, it looks like any other flame flickering gently in devotion. But its story is far from ordinary.

Legend has it that this flame has never been extinguished. Even during storms, when winds howl and violent weather threatens, the lamp miraculously reignites. Some believe it is the divine will of Lord Shiva, protecting this sacred land from the forces of time and nature. Others attribute it to the careful tending of the temple priests, who have preserved the flame with unwavering devotion over the centuries.

## 6. Connection to Kailash – A Gateway to Another Realm?

The Murudeshwar Temple, nestled on the ancient shores of Karnataka, is more than just a sanctuary for worship. It is a place imbued with legends, one of which suggests that it serves as a spiritual gateway to Kailash, Lord Shiva's mythical abode. This belief has attracted sages, mystics, and seekers of truth for centuries.

Imagine standing in the temple, with the vast Arabian Sea spread out before you and the towering Shiva statue behind you. The air hums with an indescribable energy, and time seems to slow down. For those who meditate here, the experience is often profound. Many claim to have had visions–flashes of brilliant light, fleeting glimpses of the supernatural peaks of Kailash, or even the divine presence of Lord Shiva himself. Others describe an overwhelming sense of peace, as if they have transcended the mundane world for a moment. Legends say that Murudeshwar is built on a unique energy point where the cosmic vibrations align perfectly, connecting the Earth to the divine. Ancient scriptures hint that this temple is one of the sacred gateways to Kailash, a place where mortal beings can briefly bridge the gap between the earthly realm and the eternal.

# The Miraculous Shiva Lingam that Turns Ghee into Butter

## Shivagange Temple – Karnataka (Tumkur)

**Is Ghee turning into butter?**

Located 54 kilometers from Bangalore and 19 kilometers from Tumkur, there is a mountain peak that rises 4,559 feet above sea level. This is Shivagange, a Hindu pilgrimage site situated in Dobbaspet. The mountain itself is shaped like a Shiva Lingam, and nearby, a waterfall named 'Ganga' flows forcefully, which is how this place got its name – Shivagange.

It is also known as the "South Kashi" because the number of steps leading to the peak of the mountain is the same as that of Varanasi. Shivagange houses several temples, such as the Gangadhareshwar Temple, Shri Honnammadevi Temple, Sharadambe Temple, and pilgrimage sites like Agasthya Tirtha, Kanva Tirtha, Kapila Tirtha, and Paatala Gange. At the top of this steep rock, a magnificent statue of Nandi (the bull) has been carved, showcasing Indian architecture. During the 16th century, Shivappa Nayaka strengthened this hill, and later, Kempe Gowda, the founder of Bangalore, made improvements to the fortifications.

For over 1,600 years, something fascinating has been happening during the abhishek (ritual bathing) at Shivagange Temple. Devotees have witnessed a miracle. When ghee is poured over the Shiva Lingam, it turns into butter. It is believed that this butter has medicinal properties that can cure various ailments. While most people are familiar with the process of turning **butter from ghee**, here it is reversed–the ghee transforms into butter, an extraordinary occurrence that can only be witnessed at this temple. While this is regarded as a miracle of Lord Shiva's power, the reasons behind it have been a subject of speculation for more than a century, but no scientific explanation has yet been satisfactory.

Many say that when ghee is mixed with a little water and rubbed continuously on the stone, it transforms into a butter-like substance, resembling whipped cream. Some people believe that when ghee is rubbed on stones like Shaligram, it turns into something like butter, and they have even displayed this phenomenon at their homes. Though the change of ghee into butter is a chemical process and therefore irreversible, it can still be achieved on an industrial scale.

It is also said that there is a secret tunnel running from the temple's sanctum to the Gavi Gangadhareshwar Temple [*See* Chapter 31], which is about 50 kilometers away. Another intriguing aspect of this temple is that every year during Makar Sankranti, the evening sunlight passes through the horns of Nandi and directly falls on the Shiva Lingam, illuminating the main idol located inside the cave.

Sree Padmanabhaswamy Temple - Kerala (Thiruvananthapuram)

Modhera Sun Temple - Gujarat (Mehsana)

# Sun's Rays Indicate the Month of the Year

## Vidya Shankar Temple – Karnataka
### (Chikmagalur)

Historical records suggest that the construction of the Vidya Shankar Temple was completed in the year 1338 CE, making it about 685 years old. The temple was built by two brothers, Harihara and Bukka, who constructed it in memory of their guru, Shri Vidyaranya Rishi, after his demise. The Vidya Shankar Temple is considered as significant as the four sacred Dhams and the twelve Jyotirlingas in Hinduism. This temple is situated in the same town, Sringeri, where Adi Guru Shankaracharya had established the sacred Sringeri Math.

The Vidya Shankar Temple, located in the Sringeri taluk of Chikmagalur district in Karnataka, is not just an ordinary temple, but a marvel of architectural carving and special design, combining artistry and spirituality in a unique way.

Around the temple complex, there are five different types of smaller temples, with the Vidya Shankar Temple being the most prominent. Inside its sanctum, the Shiva Lingam is worshipped as the Vidya Shankar Shiva Lingam. To the left of the Shiva Lingam is a statue of Vidya Ganapati carved on a black stone, and to the right, there is a statue of Goddess Durga.

The outer walls of the Vidya Shankar Temple are adorned with numerous unique carvings. These include depictions of gods and goddesses from the six sects defined by Adi Shankaracharya, such as Lord Shiva, Goddess Parvati, Lord Vishnu, Goddess Lakshmi, Lord

Ganesha, and Surya Dev (Sun God), among others. The carvings show the deities in various postures, which are said to represent different aspects of life and cosmic forces.

> The primary attraction of the Vidya Shankar Temple is its solar symbols, which are engraved on the 12 pillars of the temple's outer walls. These 12 pillars represent the 12 zodiac signs of the year. Technically, the size of each pillar is not identical. However, the design of these pillars, based on astronomical concepts, aligns perfectly with the celestial positions of the 12 zodiac signs. Every morning, when the sun's rays enter the temple, they hit a particular pillar that corresponds to the zodiac sign of that month, indicating the time of the year. It is believed that the pillars were constructed using astronomical principles, making this temple an engineering marvel.
>
> The temple's architecture and intricate carvings are a marvel in themselves. Whether it's the interior or exterior, every section of the temple features detailed depictions of deities, animals, and birds, carved with exquisite precision. Additionally, the columns include intricate carvings of lions standing on two legs, with stone balls held between their growling faces. Interestingly, these stone balls can be moved by hand.

# The Mystery of the Temple Vault that Cannot be Opened

## Sri Padmanabhaswamy Temple – Kerala (Thiruvananthapuram)

Standing like a fort in the center of Kerala's capital, Thiruvananthapuram, the Padmanabhaswamy Temple is filled with countless mysteries. The city is named after its presiding deity, Lord Ananta Padmanabhaswamy, who is depicted reclining on the Ananta serpent. The term "Tiru" in Tamil and Malayalam means "Shri," and "Ananta" refers to the divine serpent upon which Lord Vishnu rests. As he reclines on the divine serpent Anantanag, he is known and worshipped as Ananta Padmanabhaswamy. The prefix 'Shri' (Tiru) has been added in front of their name because it is the name of Goddess Lakshmi, and in Sanatan Dharma, deities are referred to by their names along with their consorts, like Sita-Ram/Uma-Maheshwar.

The temple features a unique statue of Lord Vishnu reclining on the serpent Ananta. This form of Lord Vishnu is mentioned in the Padma Purana, which also describes the temple's sacredness.

A mythological story connects the temple to the Mahabharata era. According to the legend, during the Dvapara Yuga, Lord Krishna's elder brother, Balarama, performed a ritual at the Padmanabhaswamy Temple on the Ekadashi of the first day of the Kali Yuga.

This mythological association highlights the temple's ancient and sacred significance. For this reason, the temple is counted among Lord Vishnu's 108 sacred shrines. According to the Hindu lunar calendar, the seventh month Ashvin marks Padmanabhaswamy Ekadashi, when special rituals are conducted at the temple.

> The Padmanabhaswamy Temple gained widespread attention in the early 21st century, especially in the first two decades. However, in the past four years, a strange silence has surrounded the temple, as its secrets remain hidden. The mystery involves the temple's vaults, which are believed to contain untold treasures. Estimates suggest the temple's treasure could be worth one trillion dollars, equating to approximately 84 lakh crore rupees. To date, treasures worth 1.32 lakh crore rupees have been found in the five opened vaults.

The temple's treasure mystery is rooted in historical events, as neighboring states like Mysore made several attempts to invade the Travancore region, but none succeeded. There are references in history suggesting that attempts to steal the temple's treasures led to mysterious deaths. This raises the question of why the sixth vault is still sealed.

> The sixth vault has generated much speculation. One belief is that opening it would lead to the temple's destruction, with catastrophic consequences that are unimaginable. Some say the vault's path leads to the sea, while others believe invisible forces guard it. The entrance of this vault is adorned with carvings of serpents. In the 1990s, a gang of thieves attempted to open the vault but fled after seeing the pair of snakes carved on the door.
>
> It is said that the vault's door is locked with a magical serpentine curse, which can only be opened by a siddha (perfected) saint using a Garuda mantra. However, the condition is that the mantra must be chanted with the same tonal frequency in which the vault was sealed. If not done correctly, the door will neither open nor break, and any attempts to force it open will result in destruction. This belief has been passed down for centuries, and the mystery remains unsolved.

## What was found in the 5 opened vaults:

**Vault-A:** In this single vault, 1,02,000 different types of diamonds and jewels were found.

**Vault-B:** In this vault, the number of jewels found was 1,469, while.

**Vault-C:** In the third vault, 617 kinds of diamonds and jewels were found.

**Vault-D and E:** The fourth and fifth vaults contained the fewest jewels, with only 40 pieces found.

The jewels recovered from the 5 vaults of the temple were special offerings made for the temple. These included long chains, large thrones, and heavy idols of Lord Padmanabhaswamy. Among the gold and silver ornaments, many diamonds were set. It is believed that there were many gold seals from BC times. This means the collection of jewels in the temple vaults has been ongoing for over 2,500 years. The total value of these items is estimated to be 1.32 lakh crore INR (about 1 trillion dollars).

# Mysterious light 'Makaravilakku'

## Sabarimala Temple – Kerala
### (Thiruvananthapuram)

This temple is considered nearly 800 years old, and the controversy regarding women's entry here is also decades-old. It is believed that Lord Ayyappa is considered a celibate (Naishthika Brahmachari), which is why women between the ages of 10 to 50 are forbidden from entering the temple. To visit the temple and have the darshan (divine sight) of Lord Ayyappa, devotees must prepare for 41 days, a practice known as Mandala Vrat. When visiting, it is mandatory to carry a small cloth bag called "Pallikettu," containing offerings like jaggery, coconut, and rice.

This temple is one of India's most famous temples. Every day, a large number of people visit the temple. Located 175 km from the capital of Kerala, Thiruvananthapuram, it sits at an altitude of about 1,000 meters above sea level. It is considered the second-largest pilgrimage in the world, with millions of devotees visiting annually. According to religious legend, during the churning of the ocean (Samudra Manthan), Lord Shiva was enchanted by Lord Vishnu's Mohini avatar, and as a result, a child was born, raised by King Rajasekhara for 12 years. Ayyappa also defeated the demoness Mahishi.

The Sabarimala Temple is situated in the Pathanamthitta district of Kerala, in a protected forest area of the Western Ghats. The temple's gates will open on the evening of November 16 for a two-month pilgrimage period. The temple is located 1,574 feet above sea level, surrounded by 18 hills. This pilgrimage site has been attracting millions of people from South India and other parts of the country for centuries.

The temple is dedicated to Lord Ayyappa, who is seen as a symbol of unity between Shaivism and Vaishnavism.

To reach the temple, devotees must climb 18 sacred steps, each with a different symbolic meaning. The first five steps represent the five senses (panchendriyas) of a human being – sight, sound, smell, taste and touch. The next eight steps symbolize the eight human emotions (*ashtaragas*) – *Kama* (desire), *Krodha* (anger), *Lobha* (greed), *Moha* (attachment), *Madha* (Pride), *Matsarya* (jealousy), *asuya* (envy) and dambha (boastfulness). The next three steps represent the three human qualities or trigunas (Satva, rajas and tamas), and the last two steps symbolize knowledge and ignorance.

> The temple is open only during the Malayalam calendar's first five days and again in April. The two major festivals here are 'Makaravilakku' on January 14 and 'Mandala' on November 15, attracting large crowds. Devotees must wear black or blue clothes when entering the temple. On Makar Sankranti, a bright light known as 'Makaravilakku' is visible in the dark, which many believe was lit by Lord Ayyappa.
>
> The temple is named after the ascetic woman Shabari, who fed Lord Rama berries, a symbol of devotion.

> **Where the Idol Gets Thinner Due to Hunger and temple remains closed only for 2 minutes every day to ensure regular bhog to Idol**

## Shree Krishna Temple – Kerala (Thiruvaarppu)

India is a center of faith, with many miraculous and mysterious temples, some of which even modern scientists have been unable to explain. One such temple is the Shri Krishna temple in Thiruvaarppu, Kerala. It is believed to be about 1,500 years old.

Several legends are associated with this temple. During their exile, the Pandavas worshipped the idol of Lord Krishna and offered him food. After completing their exile, the Pandavas left the idol in Thiruvaarppu as the local fishermen requested to keep it there and began worshipping it as their village deity.

However, the fishermen once faced trouble, and a sage advised them that they were not worshipping properly. The idol was then submerged in a sea lake.

A peculiar thing happens in this temple: the idol becomes thinner if food (bhog) is not offered regularly. The deity is offered food 10 times a day. If food is not offered on time, the idol begins to dry up. It is also said that the prasad (food offering) disappears mysteriously, believed to be consumed by Lord Krishna himself.

Earlier, the temple was closed during eclipse periods, but one day, devotees were shocked to see the idol drying up, and even the waistband slipped off. When this information reached Adi Shankaracharya, he came to witness this and was equally astonished. He then ordered that the temple remain open during eclipses and that food be offered to the idol at the prescribed time.

According to Adi Shankaracharya's instructions, the temple is only closed for two minutes a day. The temple is locked at 11:58 PM, and it is reopened exactly at midnight. The priest is given the key and an axe, with instructions to break the lock if it takes time, but never delay the food offering.

When the deity is being anointed, the idol's head is dried first and then the entire body is dried. This happens because the anointing process takes time, and during that time, offerings cannot be made.

> **Where Dogs are Considered Sacred and first offering of Prasad is to a dog**

## Parassini Shree Muthappan Temple – Kerala (Kannur)

Located in the village of Parasinikkadavu, about 16 km from Kannur in Kerala, the Parassini Muthappan Temple is a famous and mysterious temple of Northern Kerala. It does not follow any traditional customs of other Hindu temples.

> This temple is situated by the Valapattanam River, and it is customary for devotees to wash their feet in the holy river before entering. The temple's uniqueness lies in the fact that the two deities, Lord Shiva and Lord Vishnu, communicate directly with the devotees, answering their questions. It is believed that the spirit of Lord Shiva enters the medium, who portrays the deity Muthappan, and is able to provide clear solutions to the devotees' questions. The answers given are considered sacred, as they are believed to be spoken directly by the deity during the Theyyam performance.
>
> The deity is offered fried fish and toddy (a local alcoholic beverage). An interesting feature of this temple is that a dog is always present with the deity. Several dogs roam freely in the temple, and they are considered sacred.
>
> At the entrance of the temple, there are carvings of dogs. The first offering (prasad) is given to a dog that is always present inside the temple.

# Miraculous Rahu Temple, Where Milk Changes Colour

## Rahu Temple – Tamil Nadu (Thirunageshwaram)

Sri Naganathaswamy Temple or Rahu Sthalam is one of the 9 Navagraha temples located near Kumbhakonam, Tamil Nadu and is dedicated to Rahu.

The Presiding Deity is Lord Naganathaswamy (Lord Shiva). There are two Shrines for the Goddess; Piraiyanivanudalumai's Shrine is adjacent to Naganathaswamy's shrine and Giri Gujambika with Lakshmi and Saraswathy by her side.

During the churning of the ocean, a demon named Rahu disguised himself as a god and sat in the line of gods to taste the nectar. Just as he was about to drink the nectar, the incident came to the notice of Lord Vishnu, who had assumed the form of Mohini. He then cut off Rahu's head with his Sudarshan Chakra. Since then, Rahu is worshiped as a headless body, and his torso is worshiped as Ketu. According to astrology, Rahu and Ketu are also included among the nine planets. Both of them are shadow planets.

The colour of milk changes: Here, devotees offer milk (abhrishakam) on the idol of Rahu. It is said that as soon as the milk is offered to their idol, the milk changes colour and turns blue. Milk is offered on Rahu's idol. However, the mystery of how this happens remains unsolved.

**Temple built by stacking up stones without using any concrete or binding material and which appears to be suspended in air**

## Kakanmath Temple – Madhya Pradesh (Morena)

This temple, dedicated to Lord Shiva, is located in the village of Sihoniya, 65 kilometers from Gwalior in Madhya Pradesh. The uniqueness of this temple lies in its construction, which even astonishes scientists.

There are different stories associated with the Kakanmath Temple. Some say the temple was built in the 11th century by King Kachwaha Kirtiraj for his wife. It is believed that Queen Kakanwati was a great devotee of Lord Shiva. Since there were no Shiva temples nearby, the queen faced difficulty in worshipping Lord Shiva, and thus, the king built this Shiva temple. Hence, the temple was named after Queen Kakanwati.

> The temple is 115 feet tall and was built by stacking stones upon stones, without using any concrete or binding material like mortar. Today, looking at this temple, it seems like it could fall with a strong gust of wind, but despite enduring several fierce winds and storms over the years, it still stands firmly. Even in today's era of advanced technology, constructing such a tall structure with this kind of craftsmanship seems almost impossible.
>
> Some people believe this temple is cursed by ghosts. The thousand-year-old temple is said to have been built by ghosts in just one day at the behest of Lord Shiva. After completing it,

the ghosts are said to have fled at dawn, leaving the construction incomplete. As a result, the temple was built without lime or mortar, and the stones appear to be suspended in mid-air.

Also, looking at this temple, it seems like it could collapse any moment. However, it is astonishing that even the fiercest storms have been unable to shake it. Moreover, when any tourist or person tries to take stones that have fallen around the temple, the temple begins to shake. Upon seeing this, the person, filled with fear, leaves the stone right there. The surprising thing is that such stones are not found in the surrounding areas.

When scientists examined this temple, they too were baffled at how the stone structure was built without lime and mortar. Additionally, this temple has stood in the same place for thousands of years. Although this temple is not included in the Seven Wonders of the World, its construction remains a mystery. Even tourists who visit this temple are left in awe.

# Temple Where a Plate Filled with Liquor and placed near the deity's face becomes Empty in An Instant

## Kal Bhairav Temple – Madhya Pradesh (Ujjain)

Kal Bhairav Temple is a Hindu temple located in the city of Ujjain, Madhya Pradesh, India. It is dedicated to Kal Bhairav, the guardian deity of the city. Situated on the banks of the Kshipra River, it is one of the most active temples in the city, attracting hundreds of devotees every day. Liquor is one of the offerings made to the deity at this temple.

Ujjain, the city of Mahakal, is known for the presence of Lord Shiva in every particle of the land. Miracles happen every day in this sacred city. The Kshipra River, which flows here, is considered to be a river that bestows salvation (moksha). According to religious texts, Ujjain provides liberation from the cycle of birth and death to its devotees. People come from far and wide, without worrying about their difficulties, because they are eager to meet the divine form of Lord Shiva and witness the miracle of liquor being consumed at the temple.

This temple, located in the Bhairavgarh area of Ujjain, houses Lord Shiva in his Bhairav form. Although the Bhairav form of Lord Shiva is known for being wrathful and dominated by the tamasic quality, Kal Bhairav listens to the pitiful calls of his devotees and rushes to their aid.

> At this temple, the main offering is liquor. The priest pours the liquor offered by the devotees onto a plate and places it near the deity's face. Miraculously, the offering appears to be consumed by Lord Bhairavnath right before the eyes of the devotees.

> This is such a miracle that even after witnessing it, it becomes hard to believe. The plate filled with liquor empties in an instant.

Additionally, whenever a devotee wins a case in court, they come to offer a sweet made of condensed milk (mawa) as prasad to Baba. Similarly, if a devotee is blessed with a child after years of longing, they offer gram flour laddus and churma to Baba. Regardless of the type of prasad, every devotee who visits Baba's court comes with some problem, and Baba Kal Bhairav removes their difficulties with his blessings.

There is another miraculous feature at this temple that draws the attention of the devotees, and that is the deepstambh (lamp pillar) situated in the temple complex. It is believed that lighting the lamps in this pillar fulfills all wishes. Devotees also light lamps here with the wish of getting married soon. Those whose wishes are fulfilled light the lamps in the deepstambh.

Moreover, inside the temple, devotees light lamps according to their specific wishes. For example, those who seek liberation from the obstacles of enemies or wish for good health light mustard oil lamps, while those desiring an increase in their honour and reputation light jasmine oil lamps. There are two aartis (rituals) held daily at the temple – one at 8:30 AM and the other at 8:30 PM. Since Ujjain is the city of Mahakal, Kal Bhairav is also referred to as the commander-in-chief of the city.

For the devotees of Baba Kal Bhairav, the Bhairav Temple in Ujjain is no less than a pilgrimage site. It is said that without visiting this temple, the worship of Mahakal is considered incomplete.

Aghoris, who wait for the occasion of Kal Bhairav's Kalashtami (Bhairav Ashtami) to worship their deity, do so with great devotion. Likewise, regular devotees also make sure to visit the temple on this day, bow their heads, and receive blessings. The eighth day of the Krishna Paksha (dark fortnight) in the month of Margashirsha (Aghan) is known as Kal Bhairav Ashtami, which marks the birth of Kal Bhairav.

It is said that if someone visits Ujjain and worships Mahakal but does not visit Kal Bhairav, they will receive only half of the benefit of the darshan of Mahakal.

# A Temple that is an Unparalleled Example of Architecture and Design

## Khajuraho Temples – Madhya Pradesh (Chhatarpur)

Khajuraho, though a small town in the Chhatarpur district of Madhya Pradesh, is one of the most visited tourist destinations in India, second only to the Taj Mahal. Khajuraho is an unparalleled example of Indian Aryan architecture and design. The Chandela rulers commissioned the construction of these temples between 900 and 1130 CE. The earliest historical references to these temples are from the works of Abu Rayhan al-Biruni (1022 CE) and the Arab traveler Ibn Battuta. The art-loving Chandela kings built around 84 unique and incomparable temples, but so far, only 22 of these temples have been discovered. These temples are associated with the Shaiva, Vaishnava, and Jain traditions.

This region was known by different names in ancient times–Vatsa, in the medieval period as Jaijakbhukti, and after the 14th century, it came to be known as Bundelkhand.

Khajuraho was also known in ancient times as Khajurapura and Khajuravahika. The name Khajuraho came about because there were many date-palm trees in the area.

The temple's magnificent artwork and impressive sculptures led to it being included in the list of UNESCO World Heritage Sites.

> This magnificent Khajuraho temple complex contains around 246 sculptures inside and 646 sculptures outside, most of which depict eroticism. People from all over the world come here every day to witness this unique artistry.
>
> The temples of Khajuraho are an extraordinary example of art, showcasing around 10% erotic and sexual imagery. Through these sculptures, Tantra attempted to link sexuality with spirituality, and to some extent, they were successful in doing so. The sculptures of Khajuraho stand as unparalleled evidence of this. The most unique aspect of the Khajuraho sculptures is that despite depicting naked sexual acts, there is nothing in them that would cause discomfort or shame.

The temple group of Khajuraho is also remarkable for its grand ceilings (Jagati) and functionally effective plans. The sculptures here, in addition to religious images, include depictions of family life, deities, directional gods, apsaras (celestial nymphs), and beautiful maidens. The costumes and jewellery displayed here are exquisite and captivating.

## Group of Temples of Khajuraho

**Parvati Temple** – This temple is dedicated to Goddess Ganga, the goddess of rivers, who is depicted standing on her vehicle, a crocodile. This temple represents Gauri, a form of Goddess Parvati.

**Vishwanath Temple** – Located near Chhatarpur in Madhya Pradesh, this temple is dedicated to Lord Shiva and is considered one of the most extraordinary temples of Khajuraho. The temple is built in the Panchatan style, and its construction dates back to 1002-1003 CE.

**Nandi Temple** – This famous temple is dedicated to Nandi, the vehicle of Lord Shiva, and it has 12 pillars. The statue inside is 2.20 meters long. It is positioned facing the Vishwanath Temple.

**Surya Temple** – Known for its exceptional artwork, this famous Khajuraho temple houses the temple of Chitragupta, dedicated to Lord Surya (the Sun God). Here, there is a seven-foot-tall statue of Lord Surya, who drives a chariot drawn by seven horses.

**Lakshmana Temple** – The Lakshmana Temple is extremely famous and is also known as the Ramachandra Chaturbhuj Temple. It houses a highly attractive statue of Lord Surya, about 7 feet tall. This temple was built during the reign of King Yashovarman.

**Devi Jagdamba Temple** – This temple is located to the north of the Kandariya Mahadev Temple. The architecture of this temple is commendable, featuring a coiled and extremely intricate design. Erotic sculptures are also present in this temple.

**Kandariya Mahadev Temple** – The Kandariya Mahadev Temple is the largest temple in Khajuraho and is primarily dedicated to Lord Shiva. The temple was built in 999 CE. Standing at a height of 31 meters, it is the tallest temple in Khajuraho. This temple contains around 872 sculptures depicting eroticism, each approximately 1 meter tall. Made of sandstone, the temple's shine is a result of extensive polishing using leather.

**Parshvanath Temple** – Among all the ancient Jain temples in Khajuraho, the Parshvanath Temple is the most beautiful, grand, and magnificent. It is unique in its layout. Originally, this temple was dedicated to the first Jain Tirthankara.

**Vamana Temple** – This temple is dedicated to the Vamana incarnation of Lord Vishnu. The layout includes a seven-tiered structure, a sanctum, a vestibule, a large hall (Mahamanap), and a porch. The sanctum is continuous, and a four-armed Vamana statue is enshrined there.

**Matangeshwar Temple** – Built by King Harshavarman in 920 CE, this temple is considered the oldest among all the temples built by the Chandela kings in Khajuraho. It is the only one among the ancient temples where worship is still conducted.

# Temple Where a Lamp is lit with Water not with oil

## Gadiya ghat Mata Temple – Madhya Pradesh (Shajapur)

The Gadiya ghat Mata Temple in Madhya Pradesh is known for a unique phenomenon. Located on the banks of the Kali Sindh River, this temple does not require ghee or oil to light a lamp. Instead, the lamp burns with water. People come from far and wide to witness this extraordinary event. For the last five years, lamps have been lit with water at this temple.

This temple, famous by the name Gadiya ghat Mata Ji, is located near the village of Gadiya, about 15 kilometers from Nal Khera village in Agar-Malwa, on the banks of the Kali Sindh River.

> The priest, Siddho Singh Ji, who performs the rituals at the temple, explains that earlier, oil lamps were always used here. However, about five years ago, Mata appeared to him in a dream and instructed him to light the lamp with water.
>
> The next morning, he filled a lamp with water from the flowing Kali Sindh River and lit a match to the cotton wick in the lamp. As soon as the match touched the wick, the lamp miraculously lit up.
>
> This left the priest astonished, and for nearly two months, he did not share this event with anyone. Later, when he told some villagers, they initially didn't believe it. However, when they

tried filling the lamp with water themselves and lit the wick, the lamp also lit up. Since then, water from the Kali Sindh River has been used to light the lamps in this temple.

It is said that when the water is poured into the lamp, it transforms into a sticky substance, allowing the lamp to burn.

However, the water-burning lamp does not function during the monsoon season. This is because the water level of the Kali Sindh River rises during the rains, submerging the temple and making worship impossible.

After this, on the first day of the Sharadiya Navratri, which falls in September or October, the lamp is lit again with water, and it continues to burn until the next rainy season.

# Where Evidence of Ashwatthama's Arrival is Found

## Asireshwar Shiv Temple – Madhya Pradesh (Burhanpur)

According to ancient beliefs, Ashwatthama, the son of Dronacharya, is still alive today. A temple in Madhya Pradesh seems to prove this belief to be true, even after thousands of years.

Located in the Asirgarh Fort in Burhanpur district, Madhya Pradesh, a temple dedicated to Lord Shiva is believed to be the place where Ashwatthama comes every morning to worship Lord Shiva. Not only that, it is claimed that there are several pieces of evidence that support this belief.

The temple, built in the 10th century, has a fascinating history related to the Mahabharata era. What is the evidence of Ashwatthama's visit to the temple?

> The temple is often referred to as **Gupteshwar Mahadev Temple** due to the secret underground tunnel that leads to it. Near the temple, the Tapti River flows. Local people say that every morning during Brahma Muhurat, Ashwatthama takes a bath in the Tapti River and then comes to worship Lord Shiva. After offering his prayers, he returns via the secret tunnel.
>
> While the statue of Nandi Maharaj, located outside the temple, is covered with dust, the Shiva Lingam inside the temple appears

as if someone has just worshiped it. When the temple door is opened in the morning, fresh flowers and Gulal (coloured powder) are found on the Shiva Lingam. If for any reason the worship is delayed on any particular day, it seems as if the worship has already been performed. It is said that most of the time, rose petals are found on the Shiva Lingam.

**The Mysterious Cave:** Right behind the Gupteshwar Mahadev Temple is a cave, the mystery of which remains unsolved to this day. It is claimed that Ashwatthama enters the temple through this cave every day to offer his prayers and also leaves through it.

Some locals claim that this cave leads to the Makda State, some to the Sangwa Fort, and others say it leads to the Charuva Fort. However, the exact location where the cave opens is still unknown, and no one can figure out where it leads. To prevent anyone from getting lost, the cave's entrance is kept closed. It is primarily because of this mysterious cave that the temple is called the **Gupteshwar Mahadev Temple.**

**The Temple Where the Soil is believed to be Miraculous and heals wounds caused by poisonous creatures**

## Maa Ratangarh Wali Temple – Madhya Pradesh (Ratangarh)

The Maa Ratangarh Wali Temple is located in the dense forests of Ratangarh, Madhya Pradesh. This temple is also mysterious because the miracles that occur here are beyond the understanding of science.

> The biggest miracle at this temple is that if someone is bitten by a poisonous creature like a snake or a lizard, they can come here for treatment. A little bit of soil from the temple, offered in the name of Maa, is applied to the wound of the patient, and within a short time, the patient is completely healed. The poison from the venomous creature leaves their body.

This event at the temple astonishes everyone. However, it is believed to be the grace of Maa Jagdamba.

# The Temple with Tantra-Mantra

## Chausath Yogini Temple – Madhya Pradesh (Morena)

The Chausath Yogini Temple, located in Morena, Madhya Pradesh, is famous for being known as the "Tantric University." It is renowned worldwide for its practices related to tantra and mantra.

India has many temples dedicated to various deities, but some of these are considered mysterious due to their beliefs. It is true that when something becomes mysterious, the curiosity to know more about it increases significantly. In Sanatan Dharma, the concepts of tantra, mantra, and yantra are accepted. The temple we are about to discuss is known as a Tantric University. This temple is the **Chausath Yogini Temple** located in Madhya Pradesh.

While there are four Chausath Yogini temples in India–two in Odisha and two in Madhya Pradesh–only one of them is considered extremely mysterious and ancient. This temple is located in Morena, Madhya Pradesh. It is the only one that remains in good condition, and tourists from all over the world visit it.

This temple has 64 rooms, and in each room, there is a Shivling (symbol of Lord Shiva). As we all know, Lord Shiva is considered the originator of the science of tantra, which is why a Shivling is installed in each room.

The temple is situated at a height of 100 feet, and to reach it, one has to climb 200 stairs. From the top, the temple looks like a flying saucer. In the center of the temple, an open pavilion has been constructed, where a large Shivling is installed. It is said that this temple is over 700 years old.

The construction of the Chausath Yogini Temple was commissioned by King Devpal of the Kachhap dynasty in 1323 CE. In the past, astrology and mathematics were taught here based on the movement of the Sun. The temple has 64 rooms, and each room housed a statue of Lord Shiva and a Yogini. This is why it is called the **Chausath Yogini Temple**. However, many of the idols have been stolen, and the remaining ones are now housed in a museum by the Government of India. The temple, with its 101 pillars, has been declared a historical monument by the Archaeological Survey of India.

Local people believe that this temple is still covered by Lord Shiva's tantric shield. It is said that no one is allowed to stay at the temple at night. After sunset, tantric practitioners come here and try to awaken the Yoginis of Lord Shiva.

# The Temple Where the Shiva Lingam Grows Annually

## Matangeshwar Mahadev Temple – Madhya Pradesh (Khajuraho)

Matangeshwar Mahadev has been included in the UNESCO World Heritage list. Historically, there is evidence of 85 temples in the area, but only 25 remain today. It is believed that this is the only living Shiva Lingam, as it grows approximately 1 inch every year and is currently about 9 feet tall above the ground. This temple was built in the 9th century.

> The Shiva Lingam's height mysteriously increases by 8 inches annually. Its height is measured every year on Kartik Purnima by the tourism department and the temple priests. It is believed to grow symmetrically above and below the ground.
>
> **The Story Behind the Shiva Lingam** – Lord Shiva (Mahadev) had a gem called Markand Mani, which he gave to Yudhishthira (one of the Pandavas). Yudhishthira then gave it to Sage Matanga, who passed it on to Harshavardhana. It is believed that Harshavardhana buried it in the ground as there was no one to take care of it, and around this gem, a Shiva Lingam began to develop naturally. The name Matangeshwar is derived from Sage Matanga. Due to the immense power of this gem, the Shiva Lingam grows like a living human being every year. It is believed that the gem is still located beneath the massive Shiva Lingam.

The temple priests say that this symbolizes the Kali Yuga, with the top moving towards heaven (Svarga Lok) and the bottom towards the netherworld (Patal Lok). When it reaches Patal Lok, the Kali Yuga will end. It is believed that Lord Shiva married Goddess Parvati in this temple.

# Siddhivinayak temple - A Temple Dedicated to Lord Ganesha

## Siddhivinayak Temple – Maharashtra (Mumbai)

The Siddhivinayak Temple, located in Prabhadevi, Mumbai, is dedicated to the Vinayak form of Lord Ganesha. This temple was built in 1801 CE. Initially, it was made of bricks and was relatively small. Later, it was reconstructed into its current grand form.

The Siddhivinayak Temple boasts 37 domes, making it a visual delight. The old temple had a hall, a sanctum, a verandah, and a water tank. Architect Sharad Athale reconstructed the temple in 1990, drawing inspiration from the temples of Rajasthan and Tamil Nadu. The old idol was remodeled and placed on a six-sided structure. The temple was equipped with three entry gates leading inside. The temple's dome was also given a new look, with its ceiling covered in gold. After three years of continuous work, the temple now presents an awe-inspiring view to Ganesha's devotees.

The Siddhivinayak Temple houses a unique sculpture of Lord Ganesha, known as Siddhivinayak. The sanctum doors are made of wood, featuring carvings of the Ashtavinayak. The idol has four arms, making it a Chaturbhuj form. The upper right hand holds a lotus, while the left holds an axe. The lower right hand holds a rosary of beads, and the left holds a bowl full of modaks. On either side of Ganesha are his consorts, Riddhi and Siddhi, representing prosperity, success, and wealth. The idol also has a third eye on its forehead and a snake coiled around its neck.

The idol is about two and a half feet tall and made from black marble, carved into a two-foot-wide piece. The temple's ceilings are adorned with gold layers. Inside the temple are two large silver mouse sculptures, with their large ears. Devotees whisper their wishes into the mouse's ears, believing that the mouse relay these wishes to Ganesha, who fulfills them.

Typically, we worship Ganesha idols with a trunk curled to the left. However, the idols with a right-curled trunk, like in the Siddhivinayak Temple, are considered Siddha Peeths. The Siddhivinayak Temple's Ganesha quickly becomes pleased and also quickly displeased. No devotee returns disappointed from this temple, as Bappa (Ganesha) fulfills their wishes.

# The Village Where Homes Don't have Main Doors

## Shani Shingnapur Temple – Maharashtra (Ahmednagar)

The famous Shani Maharaj Temple is located in a small village called Shani Shingnapur in the Ahmednagar district of Maharashtra. It is believed that the people living here are protected by Lord Shani himself.

### What is Special About Shani Shingnapur?

The unique feature of Shani Shingnapur is that the village is protected by Lord Shani himself. The people living here do not keep safes or lockers for gold, silver, or valuable items in their homes. There are no locks or even bolts on their doors, let alone main doors. Furthermore, it is said that no theft has ever occurred in this village. It is believed that anyone who attempts theft here will be punished by Lord Shani himself.

### The Story Behind the Shingnapur Temple

The Shani Dev temple in Shingnapur is one of the most famous temples, but very few people know the mystery behind the existence of the temple. The story of its existence goes like this.

Around 200 years ago, during a heavy rainfall, the village experienced a flood-like situation. During that time, a black stone idol of Lord Shani was carried by the floodwaters and got stuck near a ber (Indian Jujube) tree. Once the floodwaters receded, the villagers went out to graze cattle and discovered the black stone idol. When an attempt was made to touch the idol with a stick, blood started flowing from it. Seeing the blood, the people fled in fear and informed the entire village about the incident. All the villagers gathered to see the idol, and it was placed under the open sky.

> There is a neem tree to the north of the idol, but no branch of this tree has ever cast its shadow on the idol. If a branch comes near, it breaks off and falls before touching the idol. The stick that was used to touch the idol left a wound-like hole in the idol, which remains even today.
>
> Shani Jayanti, the celebration of Lord Shani's birth, is observed on the Amavasya (new moon) of the Jyeshtha month. It is believed that anyone suffering from the malefic effects of Shani, such as Shani's Dhaiya or Sade Sati, should visit Shani Shingnapur Temple on Shani Jayanti. Lord Shani is considered the god of justice, and anyone who performs worship properly can get rid of all their difficulties.
>
> The belief that women should not enter or touch the idol in the Shani Temple is based on the idea that Shani is not a deity but a planet, as mentioned in the Skanda Purana. From a scientific point of view, it is believed that the body of a woman is meant for procreation, and in Shani temples, rituals related to tantra-mantra and exorcism are often performed. Therefore, women should not visit places with such energy, as it might cause harm to them.
>
> In Shani Shingnapur, there are no doors on the houses because Lord Shani himself resides here. The people are not afraid of theft, as no one would want to face the wrath of Shani. As a result, people here avoid committing theft or other bad deeds, as Lord Shani, the god of justice, will punish wrongdoers.

The idol here is made of black stone and is about 5 feet tall. It is kept in the open, making it a major point of attraction for visitors. In the temple, there is a tradition of offering oil to Lord Shani, which the devotees do with great faith.

⊰ ◦ ⊱

Shree Stambheshwar Mahadev Temple - Gujarat (Bharuch)

Matsya Mata Temple - Gujarat (Valsad)

# A Temple Carved from a Single Rock

## Kailasa Temple – Maharashtra (Aurangabad)

The Kailasa Temple is located in Ellora, Aurangabad, Maharashtra. The mystery of this temple continues to be a challenge for modern science, and it is a remarkable testament to our glorious history and civilization.

The Kailasa Temple was built during the reign of Rashtrakuta King Krishna I (756-773 CE). However, there is no information available regarding the purpose, construction technology, or the name of the creator of this Shiva temple. The inscriptions on the walls of the temple are very old, and the language used is unreadable.

> Normally, when constructing a temple or building, stones are stacked one on top of the other. But in the case of Kailasa Temple, a unique method was adopted. The temple was carved out from the top of a mountain, cutting it from above to below. Just like a sculptor carves a statue from a block of stone, the Kailasa Temple was carved from a mountain.
>
> The temple, pillars, doors, carvings, etc., were created by hollowing out and cutting the stone. The design and planning behind this are mind-blowing. In addition, the system for storing rainwater, the channels for draining water, the temple tower, the bridges, finely designed and beautiful canopies, intricately crafted stairs, and secret underground passages were all created by cutting stone. This is not something ordinary.

Today, scientists and researchers estimate that approximately 400,000 tons of stone was removed to create the temple. Based on this, it is believed that if 7,000 workers worked for 150 years, the temple would have been completed. However, it is said that the Kailasa Temple was completed in just 17 years.

During that time, when there were no large cranes or advanced tools, how was so much stone cut and removed from the site? This mystery is perplexing. Was alien technology used to construct this temple? No one knows, but it certainly seems so.

In today's time, even with all the modern technology, it would be impossible to build another Kailasa Temple.

# A Temple Built by the Pandavas in One Night

## Ambreshwar Shiva Temple – Maharashtra (Ambernath)

The Ambreshwar Shiva Temple in Ambernath, Maharashtra, is a remarkable temple where it is believed that the Pandavas constructed a part of the temple in just one night. The temple houses a highly revered Shiva Linga.

This temple is also known as a Pandav-era temple.

During their exile, the Pandavas managed to complete half of the temple in one night. However, due to the arrival of the Kaurava army, they had to leave the temple unfinished. The construction of the temple was later completed in the year 1060 CE by King Mambani, as confirmed by inscriptions found on the temple.

> There is temple of Lord Ambreshwar in Ambernath. Ambreshwar Temple is known as the "Pandavkalin' temple, believed to have been constructed by the Pandavas during their period of exile. While they could only complete part of the temple in one night, the remaining portion was completed by King Mambani. The architectural marvels and the natural wonders of this temple are famous far and wide.
>
> Outside the temple, there are not one, but two Nandi statues. The temple has three entrances or "Mukhamandapas." After entering, there is another Sabha Mandapa, followed by nine steps leading down to the Garbhagriha (sanctum sanctorum).

The most fascinating and unique feature of the temple is the Shiva Linga. The main Shiva Linga is of the "Triamasti" type, and the figure of Goddess Parvati is installed on its knee. The upper part of the Linga depicts Lord Shiva in a dance pose.

Near the Garbhagriha, there is a Kund (tank) from which hot water flows. There is also a cave nearby, which is believed to be connected to Panchvati through an underground passage.

# A Temple Representing the Movement of Time

## Konark Sun Temple – Odisha (Puri)

The Konark Sun Temple, located approximately 35 kilometers (22 miles) northeast of Puri city in Odisha, India, is a 13th-century temple built around the year 1250 CE. The temple is attributed to King Narasimha Deva I of the Ganga dynasty. In 1984, UNESCO recognized it as a World Heritage Site.

The Konark Sun Temple is built in the Kalinga architectural style, which is one of the most famous architectural styles of Indian temples.

To showcase its cultural significance, the Konark Sun Temple is depicted on the reverse side of the Indian 10 rupee note. Dedicated to the Hindu Sun God, Surya, the temple complex's remnants resemble a 100-foot-high (30 meters) chariot with massive wheels and horses, all carved from stone. The temple was once more than 200 feet (61 meters) tall, but most of the structure is now in ruins.

The Konark Sun Temple is a mysterious temple in India, where no worship has ever been conducted. Built in the 13th century, it is located in the Odisha state of India. The temple follows the Kalinga style of architecture, which is one of the most renowned styles of Indian temples.

The name "Konark" is derived from two words: "Kona," meaning corner or edge, and "Arka," meaning Sun. It is believed that the temple was constructed by King Narasimha Deva I between 1236-1264 CE.

The Konark Sun Temple is the most famous sun temple in India, made from red sandstone and black granite. It is designed in the shape of Lord Surya's chariot, with 24 stone wheels and 7 horses, although only one horse remains today.

The entrance of the temple is adorned with two lions riding elephants, depicted in a protective posture. The entrance also features a Natya Mandapa, where dancers once performed before the deity.

The Konark Sun Temple is built with three mandapas (pavilions), two of which have collapsed. In the third mandapa, where the idol once stood, the British sealed the doors with sand and stone before India's independence to prevent further damage to the temple.

Inside the temple, there are three statues of Lord Surya, all carved from a single stone.

1. **Childhood Stage - Rising Sun:** 8 feet

2. **Youth Stage - Noon Sun:** 9.5 feet

3. **Mature Stage - Setting Sun:** 3.5 feet

According to several legends, it is believed that a magnetic stone was placed at the top of the temple, and due to its effect, ships passing through the sea near Konark were drawn towards it, causing them significant damage.

However, another story suggests that due to this stone, the navigational instruments on the ships could not point in the correct magnetic direction. As a result, Muslim sailors took the magnetic stone away to protect their ships. This stone was believed to have acted as a central stone that balanced all the stones in the temple walls. But after the removal of this stone, the balance was lost, and the temple's walls collapsed. However, there is no historical evidence to support the existence of such a magnetic central stone.

As the Konark Sun Temple is dedicated to Lord Surya, worship of the Sun God is carried out here. The temple is designed like a massive chariot and is known for its artistic excellence and the use of precious metals in its decoration.

The Konark Temple was initially built at the edge of the sea. Over time, the sea gradually receded, causing the temple to move farther from the shore. Due to its dark colour, it was referred to as the "Black Pagoda," and it is believed to have been used to reduce negative energy.

The statues created here are depicted with great beauty and sensuality, with many of them shown enjoying sexual pleasures. These depictions, however, are limited to the outer parts of the temple. The idea was that anyone entering the sanctum sanctorum should leave behind their worldly pleasures.

At the entrance of the Konark Temple, two large lion statues were made, with each lion symbolizing the destruction of elephants. In this context, the lion represents pride, and the elephant represents wealth.

> The Konark Sun Temple is not only famous for its design as the chariot of Lord Surya, but also for the sensual sculptures found within the temple. These figures are clearly and delicately depicted on the second level of the main entrance mandapa.

# A Temple Where the Flag at the Top of the Main Spire Waves in the Opposite Direction of the Wind

## Shri Jagannath Temple - Odisha (Puri)

The Jagannath Temple in Puri is a temple from the 11th century and one of the Char Dham temples of India, filled with excellent architecture, awe-inspiring legends, and vibrant rituals. The Jagannath Temple is a vast complex that covers an area of 400,000 square feet, containing at least 120 temples and pilgrimage sites. Its rich, intricate sculptures and high architecture make it one of the most magnificent monuments in India.

The temple is famous for the annual Rath Yatra or Chariot Festival. During the festival, large wooden representations of the three main deities are placed on huge chariots and pulled through the streets surrounding the temple. The size of these chariots, the power of the deities, and the enthusiasm of the crowd led to the English word "juggernaut."

In the 19th century, a British missionary said that he saw devotees throwing themselves under the wheels of the chariots, and thus coined the term "juggernaut" to symbolize an unstoppable force. For him, as a Christian missionary, the chariot represented an extremely powerful, violent, and dangerous force. However, this magnificent temple is not only famous for the chariot festival. It is also renowned for its mysterious and spiritual power, the many legends and beliefs surrounding it, and certain secrets that defy scientific explanation.

> The flag atop the temple's main spire waves in the opposite direction of the wind. There is no scientific explanation for this, nor for the fact that no bird or plane flies above the temple.

Adding to the temple's mysterious nature, the architecture is constructed in such a way that the temple never casts a shadow. A metal statue, called the Sudarshan Chakra, placed at the top of one of the towers, can be seen from every corner of Puri city, and it always appears to face the viewer.

When you enter the Jagannath Temple through the Singhdwar (Lion's Gate), you can hear the sound of the nearby sea waves (Puri is on the Bay of Bengal). However, after taking the first step inside, you can no longer hear the sound of the sea waves. In fact, within the temple complex, no sea sounds can be heard from anywhere.

**According to a legend, the temple's kitchen** — which serves food to 25,000 to 100,000 people daily — is presided over by Goddess Mahalaxmi. If she is displeased with the food, a dog mysteriously appears and causes all the food to burn, forcing the cooks to start preparing fresh food.

The Jagannath Temple also houses a 1,800-year-old ritual. Every day, a priest climbs the equivalent of 45 floors to change the flag. It is said that if this ritual is missed for even one day, the temple will remain closed for 18 years.

Considered one of the most ancient and sacred cities for Hindus in India, Puri in the state of Odisha is home to the Jagannath Temple. Every year, the Rath Yatra begins from the 2nd day of the Shukla Paksha in the month of Ashadha, attracting millions of devotees from across India and abroad.

**Incomplete Idols in the Temple**: This is the only temple where the idols of Lord Krishna (Jagannath), Balram, and Subhadra are incomplete and made of wood. These idols are replaced every year. The reason behind the incomplete and wooden idols is linked to a long story involving King Indradyumna and his wife Gundicha.

**Flag that Waves Against the Wind**: The red flag atop the Jagannath Temple always waves in the opposite direction of the wind. The reason for this phenomenon is yet to be explained scientifically, but it is undoubtedly a fascinating phenomenon.

Every evening, the flag is replaced by humans climbing the temple, and when the flag waves, it draws the attention of all onlookers. The flag has a crescent of Lord Shiva on it.

**No Shadow of the Dome**: Standing near the temple, it is impossible to see the shadow of its dome. The shadow of the main dome is invisible at any time of the day.

**India's Most Grand Temple**: The Jagannath Temple is the most grand and tallest temple in India. It covers an area of 400,000 square feet and has a height of around 214 feet.

**Miraculous Sudarshan Chakra**: From any place in Puri, you can always see the Sudarshan Chakra on top of the temple. It always appears to be facing you. This is also known as the Neel Chakra and is made from ashtadhatu (eight metals). It is considered to be extremely sacred.

**Opposite Wind Direction**: Normally, the wind blows from the sea to the land during the day and in the opposite direction in the evening. However, in Puri, it is reversed. Most coastal areas experience wind blowing from the sea to the land, but here, the wind blows from the land to the sea.

**No Birds Fly Above the Dome**: No birds have ever been seen flying around the dome of the temple. It is said that airplanes are not allowed to fly over the temple. Birds are never seen flying near the temple's spire, although it is common for birds to sit on or fly around the domes of most temples in India. It is also believed that if such an event occurs, it is considered an omen of an inauspicious time.

**World's Largest Kitchen**: 500 chefs, along with 300 assistants, prepare Lord Jagannath's prasadam (food offerings). The temple can serve food to up to 2 million devotees. The temple has enough food prepared for the entire year, and not a single portion of the food is wasted. It is said that the kitchen prepares food for 20,000 people daily, but on festive days, food is prepared for up to 50,000 people. If millions of people arrive, they can still partake in the prasadam.

**Strange Way of Cooking Rice**: In the temple's kitchen, seven pots are stacked one over the other, and everything is cooked on wood. In this process, the food in the top pot cooks first, and then, in succession, the food in the pots below is cooked. Isn't it a miracle!

**Sound of the Sea**: As soon as you step into the Singhdwar of the temple (inside the temple), you cannot hear the sound of the sea. However, as soon as you step outside, you can hear the sea's waves clearly. This can be experienced especially in the evening.

**Odor from Outside Doesn't Enter**: Similarly, there is a Swarg Dwar (gateway to heaven) where corpses are cremated. However, when you leave the temple, you only sense the odor of burning bodies.

**Changing Idol Forms**: Here, Lord Krishna is referred to as Jagannath. Along with him, his brother Balabhadra (Balram) and sister Subhadra reside. The idols of the three deities are made of wood. Every 12 years, the idols undergo a Navakalebara (new incarnation), and new idols are made, though their size and appearance remain the same. It is said that these idols are not worshipped but only placed for darshan (viewing).

**Non-Hindus Are Not Allowed Entry**: Non-Hindus are not allowed to enter the Jagannath Temple. It is believed that these restrictions were placed due to previous invasions and attempts to damage the temple by foreigners. The temple has been the target of damage in the past.

> **The Mysterious Temple Where it Feels Cold Even in Hot Summer Months**

## Kumhda Pahad Shiv-Parvati Temple – Odisha (Titlagarh)

One of the mysterious temples in India is located in the state of Odisha. The Titlagarh area in Odisha is considered as the hottest region of the State, and here, on a mountain called Kumhda, there is a unique temple dedicated to Lord Shiva. This temple is filled with mysteries.

> The area is known for its scorching heat due to the rocky terrain. However, what is astonishing is that despite the intense heat outside, the temple remains incredibly cool, almost like an air-conditioned room. It is very difficult for devotees to stand outside in the temple complex for more than 5 minutes due to the heat, but as soon as they step inside the temple, they experience a cool breeze that feels even more refreshing than air conditioning. The mystery behind this phenomenon remains unsolved till this day.

However, as soon as devotees step outside the temple, the intense heat is immediately felt again. Even during the hot summer months, many visitors need to use blankets inside the temple because of the cold sensation.

This miraculous Shiva temple is located in a small town called Titlagarh, in the Balangir district of Odisha.

**Titlagarh**: Titlagarh is the hottest region of eastern Odisha. Specifically, the Kumhda Mountain here remains extremely hot because it receives direct intense sunlight, and there are rocky terrains. This causes the temperature to feel even hotter. However, despite this scorching heat, when you enter the Shiva-Parvati temple here, you immediately experience the miracle of God.

This temple is an ancient, mysterious shrine of Lord Shiva and Goddess Parvati, famous for its divine consciousness and its mystery. It is a puzzle even for science. This is a temple where you feel cold even in the summer. The area outside the temple is a rocky mountain, where the heat remains constant. But inside the temple, the temperature is always pleasant.

The temple does not have any coolers or air-conditioners, yet the temperature inside the temple always remains low. Interestingly, as the outside temperature rises, the temperature inside the temple continues to stay cool.

During the months of May and June, when the outside temperature often reaches up to 55°C, the coldness inside the Titlagarh Shiva Temple actually increases.

During the summer season, it is not uncommon to need blankets inside the temple.

This temple is located on the Kumhda mountain, where the rocks get extremely hot. Yet, the temperature inside the temple remains consistently cool. Just a few steps inside the temple are enough for the entire atmosphere to change.

> **Where Just the Sight of the Deity Relieves All Sufferings of Devotees**

## Mehandipur Balaji Temple – Rajasthan (Dausa)

The Mehandipur Balaji Temple, located in the Dausa district of Rajasthan, is a Hindu temple dedicated to Lord Hanuman. This temple is not like ordinary temples; rather, it is considered a haunted and terrifying place.

Every day, thousands of people visit this temple who are believed to be possessed by evil spirits or ghosts. Ordinary people are often frightened by the sights within the temple, as some people are seen screaming loudly while others crawl on the ground. To remove the influence of ghosts, black magic, and evil spirits, a special kirtan is held at 2:00 pm every day. In this temple, it is strictly forbidden to take any prasad or any other substance outside the temple, as it is believed that doing so brings evil spirits along with you. It is said that even people who do not believe in ghosts, spirits, or black magic should visit the Mehandipur Balaji Temple at least once.

Three deities are worshipped at Mehandipur Balaji Temple. The main deity is Lord Hanuman, and in addition to him, there are also worshipped deities of Pretraj (King of ghosts) and Bhairav. The connection of these three deities with ghosts and evil spirits is believed to be significant. It is said that the idol of Lord Balaji in the temple appeared miraculously. The legends suggest that Hanuman's activities at this location began during his childhood, which is why this temple is known as Balaji Temple.

Without a doubt, this place can intimidate those with faint hearts. Upon entering the temple complex, you may experience a noticeable change in the environment around you. The architecture of the Mehandipur Balaji Temple reflects its unique history and distinctiveness. After entering the temple, you are sure to feel the presence of negativity in the surroundings.

> The temple has a total of four chambers. The first two chambers house the idols of Lord Hanuman and Bhairav, but when you enter the final chamber, you may have a terrifying experience. You may see several men and women screaming, beating themselves, and shaking their heads. Some of them may be chained with iron chains and shouting loudly.
>
> It is strictly prohibited to eat or take the prasad from the temple outside. Not only is it forbidden to carry the prasad home, but it is also not recommended to give it to anyone else. It is believed that bringing anything from this temple into your home will invite the influence of evil spirits.
>
> An interesting belief about the temple is that there is a hole in the chest of the idol of Balaji, from which water continuously flows. This is believed to be Lord Balaji's sweat.
>
> It is said that Lord Hanuman is present in his child form at this temple. Near the temple, there are idols of Lord Ram and Goddess Sita, and Lord Hanuman is believed to always keep watching over them.
>
> To protect against the influence of ghosts and spirits, a special kirtan is held at 2:00 pm daily at Pretraj Sarkar's court. The temple also houses an idol of Bhairav Baba, and it is believed that worshipping here helps to overcome negative energies.
>
> Visitors to the Mehandipur Balaji Temple are required to refrain from consuming eggs, meat, alcohol, garlic, and onions for one week.
>
> While in most temples, the sound of bells is heard, as soon as you step into the premises of the Mehandipur Balaji Temple, you will hear the loud screams of men and women. The cries of the afflicted can be quite terrifying.
>
> While other temples in India are known for offering prasad, Mehandipur Balaji Temple is unique because no prasad is offered

here. As soon as you enter the temple complex, small vendors will try to sell you prasad. It is necessary to buy a black ball, which is then moved around your body and thrown into the fire. After that, devotees seek blessings from Lord Hanuman to remove their sufferings.

# The Temple Where Goddess Takes a Fire Bath

## Idana Mata Temple – Rajasthan (Udaipur)

Located 60 kilometers away from Udaipur in the Aravalli hills, the Idana Mata Temple is a very mysterious place because, every month in the early morning, fire spontaneously ignites 2-3 times, and the cause of the fire has never been identified. This temple, which is situated 65 kilometers from Udaipur city on the Kurabad-Bambora road, is an ancient Shakti Peeth dedicated to Idana Mata. The temple has a very unique characteristic that astounds everyone.

> The temple does not have a roof, and when the fire breaks out, everything except the idol of the goddess, including her adornments and cloth, is burned down. This fire is considered to be the goddess's "Agni Snan" (Fire Bath), and it is believed that whenever the idol's adornments and cloth become too heavy, the goddess herself ignites the fire to purify herself. In this fire, only the cloth and adornments on the idol burn to ashes, and nothing else in the temple is harmed by the flames.
>
> This temple is famous for the goddess, Idana Mata, performing her Agni Snan. The fire ignites suddenly on its own and then cools down by itself. The flames of this fire are not small; they can be seen from up to 5 kilometers away.
>
> However, no one has been able to determine how this fire starts, nor is there any set time for when it occurs.

Devotees from all over the country come here to witness the goddess's Agni Snan and seek her blessings. It is believed that anyone who witnesses the Agni Snan feels incredibly fortunate and blessed. A large crowd of devotees gathers to watch this event. A festive atmosphere fills the area, and the temple is filled with the chants of devotees praising the goddess.

It is also said that when the goddess is pleased, she performs her Agni Snan. Idana Mata is worshipped by the royal families of Rajasthan as their family deity. At this temple, devotees offer colourful cloth (Lachha Chunari) and tridents (Trishul) to the goddess.

When the fire begins to ignite gently, the priest removes the goddess's jewellery and places it aside. This is because everything around the goddess in the temple burns to ashes, except for the idol of Idana Mata. Once the fire cools down, the goddess is adorned again. There are also beliefs that people suffering from paralysis (Lakwa) are completely healed when they visit this temple.

# The Temple of Rats

## Karni Mata Temple – Rajasthan (Bikaner)

The Karni Mata Temple, located in Bikaner (Rajasthan), is a very unique temple. Around 20,000 black rats live here, and millions of tourists and devotees visit this temple to fulfill their wishes.

Karni Devi, believed to be an incarnation of Goddess Durga, is worshipped in this temple, which is also called the "Temple of Rats." The rats here are referred to as "Kabas," and they are fed with reverence. If a rat runs over your feet, it is considered a blessing from the goddess, and if you see a white rat, it is believed that your wish will be fulfilled.

The prasadam offered in the temple is considered to be the "leftover" food of the rats. However, till date, there have been no reports of any diseases spreading due to the rats.

There are thousands of rats in the temple, some of which are white, and it is believed that these white rats are manifestations of Karni Mata and her sons. This is why the rats in the temple are considered sacred and are worshipped.

The thousands of rats in this temple are believed to be the descendants of Karni Mata, and thus harming a rat is considered a serious sin. To ensure no rats are harmed, devotees are advised not to lift their feet but to drag them while walking inside the temple. If, by mistake, a rat is killed by a devotee, they are required to make amends. This is considered very unlucky and a grave sin. In such a case, the devotee must offer a silver or gold rat, weighing the same as the deceased rat, to the temple.

Karni Mata is the family deity of the royal families of Bikaner and Jodhpur. People from Bikaner and Jodhpur also consider her as their family deity and worship her.

This temple is unique not just because of the rats but because of the fact that there are more rats than idols in the temple. According to the temple priests, there are over 30,000 rats here.

# Temple which could not be damaged by Pakistan's bombs in 1965 war

## Tanot Mata Temple – Rajasthan (Jaisalmer)

The Tanot Mata Temple, located near the Pakistan border, is said to be the last Hindu temple at the Indian border. It is said that the union of Shiva and Shakti created the world, and for its continuance, the balance of Shiva-Shakti is necessary. In the Sanatan Dharma, the worship of both Shiva and Shakti is of special importance. While there are many temples dedicated to goddesses across the country, the Tanot Mata Temple is one such place where even Pakistani generals bow their heads.

Tanot Mata Temple, located near the Pakistan border, is the last Hindu temple on Indian soil. The border with Pakistan is just 20 kilometers away from the temple. The operation of the temple has traditionally been in the hands of people or priests, but this particular temple is managed by Border Security Force (BSF) personnel. The BSF soldiers are responsible for maintaining the temple, as well as conducting the three daily aratis with devotion and enthusiasm.

During the India-Pakistan war, an event occurred that made the Pakistani soldiers realize their mistake and retreat after bowing their heads before the goddess. It is said that Pakistani soldiers attacked the temple from three different locations but were unsuccessful in their attempts.

## TEMPLE WHICH COULD NOT BE DAMAGED BY PAKISTAN'S BOMBS IN 1965 WAR

In 1965, during the war, Pakistani forces dropped around 3,000 bombs on the temple, but not a single bomb caused any damage. Even though approximately 450 bombs fell inside the temple's premises, none of them exploded. Today, these unexploded bombs are kept safely in the temple's museum.

Witnessing this miracle, Pakistan's then officer Brigadier Shah Nawaz Khan was left astonished and, upon seeking permission from the Indian government, presented a silver canopy (Chhatra) to the goddess.

# The Temple with an 80-Ton Heavy Stone on Its Summit

## Brihadeeswara Temple (Rajarajeswara Temple) – Tamil Nadu (Thanjavur)

For those who consider modern-day engineering to be the best, the Brihadeeswarar Temple in Tamil Nadu is a must-know. This temple, which is nearly 1,000 years old, is designed in a way that even today, scientists and engineers are astonished when they see it.

The temple stands 66 meters tall, equivalent to about 13 stories. Despite its height, the temple was constructed without a foundation, meaning it was built directly on the earth's surface. A staggering 130,000 tons of granite stone were used in the construction of the temple. However, it is remarkable that there is no granite found in the vicinity of the temple. One might wonder how such large quantities of granite were transported to this site.

Another mystery of the temple's architecture is that, despite its height, no cement or adhesive substances like mud were used in its construction. Yet, it has withstood natural disasters like storms, earthquakes, and tsunamis for centuries and remains standing firm.

At the top of the temple, there is an 80-ton dome made from a single piece of stone. This massive stone dome was placed at such a height without the use of a crane. The even more astonishing fact is that it was constructed in such a way that its shadow never touches the ground.

The architectural brilliance of this temple, built thousands of years ago, suggests that the engineering techniques of the ancient world were far more advanced than we think, even when compared to modern-day technology.

The famous Brihadeeswarar Temple, dedicated to Lord Shiva, is located in Thanjavur, Tamil Nadu. This 1,000-year-old temple is listed as a UNESCO World Heritage Site. It is the world's first and only temple entirely built from granite stones. Brihadeeswarar Temple is also known as Brihadeeswar or Rajarajeswara Temple.

One of the largest temples in India, the construction of Brihadeeswarar Temple was initiated by the Chola emperor Rajaraja Chola I after he received divine inspiration in a dream. The temple's construction began between 1003-1010 CE. Standing at 13 stories, the temple reaches a height of 66 meters and is built on a 16-feet high solid platform.

The Chola rulers named this temple Rajarajeswar, but it was later renamed Brihadeeswar by the Maratha rulers who invaded Thanjavur. The primary deity of the temple is Lord Shiva, and inside the main temple, there is a 12-feet tall Shiva Linga. This temple is an exemplary example of Dravidian architecture. The construction of the main temple and its gopurams (gateway towers) dates back to the 11th century, though the temple has undergone several expansions, repairs, and restorations over the centuries.

In the 16th and 17th centuries, under the Nayak kings, shrines dedicated to Lord Kartikeya (Murugan Swami), Goddess Parvati (Amman), and the statue of Nandi were added to the temple. The temple also contains inscriptions in both Sanskrit and Tamil.

Brihadeeswarar Temple is a magnificent example of ancient engineering and architecture. The summit of the temple, or the dome, is constructed in such a way that its shadow never touches the ground. The dome itself weighs a massive 80,000 kilograms and is made from a single piece of stone.

How this 80-ton stone was transported to the top of the temple remains a mystery. It is believed that a 1.6-kilometer long ramp was built, and the stone was gradually moved inch by inch to the top of the temple.

A total of 130,000 tons of stone were used in the construction of Brihadeeswarar Temple, and it took a mere 7 years to complete the temple — an extraordinary achievement given the time period. The speed of the construction and the sheer scale of the project, with the technology available back then, is still a mystery to modern-day engineers.

Granite stones are so hard that cutting and carving them requires special diamond-tipped tools. The fact that intricate, artistic sculptures and carvings were made out of these stones during that era, without modern tools, is a true wonder.

Inside the temple's gopuram, the statue of Nandi (the sacred bull of Lord Shiva) is another remarkable feat. This statue measures 16 feet long, 8.5 feet wide, and 13 feet tall, with a weight of 20,000 kilograms. The specialty of this statue is that it is made from a single piece of stone. This statue is the second-largest Nandi statue in India.

The question of how such enormous quantities of stone were transported from such long distances to the temple construction site remains unanswered. There are no mountains in the vicinity from which the stones could have been sourced. The sheer scale of the construction, combined with the fact that no one knows how such large stones were moved, makes Brihadeeswarar Temple a true marvel of ancient engineering.

> **Temple Where the Weight of the Idol Increases and Decreases on its own as it is taken out or brought back**

## Kal Garuda Temple – Tamil Nadu (Nachiar Koil)

The stone Garuda (the stone eagle), which is the vehicle of Lord Vishnu, is an intriguing feature of this temple. When it is taken out in a procession from the temple, it is interesting to note that the weight of the stone Garuda continues to increase. However, when it is brought back into the temple, the weight fluctuates once again.

It is a mystery that the weight of the same stone idol is different in different places. This phenomenon is a real spectacle during the festival at this Vishnu temple in Tamil Nadu.

Kal Garuda, the representation of Vishnu's vehicle or mount, is the most prominent feature of this temple. It is the only stone-made vehicle among the 108 Divya Desam temples.

> To carry Kal Garuda (the stone bird) out of the temple, only four people are required. As it progresses, the number of people needed increases in multiples of 8, 16, 32, and 64 before it reaches the vehicle mantapa (hall) at the entrance of the temple. Here, Garuda is decorated with a silk dhoti, ornaments, and special floral garlands sent by the Srirangam temple. Leading the procession with the goddess, Kal Garuda begins its 6-hour journey at 7 PM, traveling along with the Perumal (Vishnu).
>
> As the procession reaches the streets outside the temple, the number of people required to carry the Kal Garuda increases to 128. The puzzle here is that no matter how many people lift

the stone idol, its weight remains the same. Otherwise, the stone would either grow bigger or its density would increase, but this does not happen. Is there some supernatural force working on the mysterious stone idol of Garuda, making its weight increase?

When the Garuda vehicle returns with the procession to the temple in the morning, the weight fluctuates again. The number of people required to carry it decreases in multiples of 128, 64, 32, 16, and 8, and eventually, only four people are needed to place it back at its original position inside the temple.

> **The temple carved out of a hill and sans any foundation - the Ellora of South India**

## Kalugumalai Vettuvan Temple – Tamil Nadu (Kovilpatti)

Many magnificent temples were built by kings in various eras across Tamil Nadu. Most of these temples are famous for their architectural splendor and grand gopurams. When a devotee visits any temple, the first thing that catches their eye is the towering gopuram of the temple.

> Usually, the construction of buildings starts from the foundation and goes up, but a temple in Tamil Nadu breaks this rule. This temple, which is built upside down without a foundation, astonishes everyone.
>
> This temple was carved out of a hill, and the interesting part is that it cannot be seen from any other place on the hill. It is known as the Ellora of South India. The architectural style and construction of this temple leave visitors in awe.

The Kalugumalai Vettuvan Temple was built in the 8th century by the Pandyas. This temple is considered even older than the Tanjore Temple in Tamil Nadu. The fascinating thing about this temple is that it was carved from a large B-shaped hill, which was cut from top to bottom. The skill of the craftsmen of that time is evident, as shaping a complete temple out of a hill is nothing short of a miracle.

Marks from chisels can still be seen on the walls and rocks of the temple, showcasing the craftsmanship of the artisans from that period. These marks suggest the immense effort and time taken to create this extraordinary structure. The gopuram of the temple houses beautiful sculptures of Dakshinamurthy, Narasimha, and Murugan. These sculptures are so intricately carved that they make the era come alive for the viewers.

This temple is dedicated to Lord Shiva, and it holds special significance for Shiva devotees. It is believed that the temple is the center of spiritual energy, providing peace and tranquility to the devotees. While sculptures are carved on the temple's vimanas and towers, the temple still appears incomplete for certain reasons. Its unfinished structure and unique style make it even more mysterious.

> # The Temple Where Lord Shiva Came to Test Goddess Parvati

## Ekambareswarar Temple – Tamil Nadu (Kanchipuram)

The Ekambareswarar Temple, one of the largest temples in the world, is located in the city of Kanchipuram, Tamil Nadu. This famous Hindu temple is dedicated to Lord Shiva and is a remarkable example of South Indian architecture.

Spanning 40 acres, this grand temple stands 11 stories high. Built in the Dravidian architectural style, it is one of the tallest temples in South India. The 59-meter-high gopuram (main entrance) of the temple was constructed by King Krishnadevaraya of the Vijayanagar dynasty.

When you enter the main courtyard of the temple, a vast corridor welcomes you. There are five such large corridors within the temple. The main sanctum houses Lord Shiva, but there is no separate temple for Goddess Parvati, as the city's Kamakshi Temple represents her.

Inside the temple is a 2.5-feet-long sand-made Shivlinga, which is not bathed with water, but instead, oil is used for the ritual. Devotees are not allowed to approach the Shivlinga directly.

The temple also houses a small statue of Lord Vishnu, known as the Vamana Murti, and it is one of the attractions of the temple.

One of the main highlights of the temple is the Aviraama Kala Mandapam, which features 1,000 pillars. These pillars are intricately carved, adding to the temple's grandeur. Along with the inner courtyard walls, 1,008 Shivlingas are also installed.

The temple complex has a beautiful pond called the Shiva Ganga Teertham, which also includes a statue of Lord Ganesha, the son of Lord Shiva, in its center.

> Behind the temple is a raised platform with a 3,500-year-old mango tree. It is believed that Goddess Parvati meditated under this tree to win Lord Shiva's favour. Pleased with her penance, Lord Shiva appeared from the mango tree, thus earning the temple its name 'Ekambareswarar,' meaning 'Lord of the Mango Tree.' A portion of the tree's trunk is preserved as a heritage artifact in the temple. The tree symbolizes the four Vedas and is said to bear mangoes with four different tastes.

# The Temple with Musical Steps

## Airavatesvara Temple – Tamil Nadu (Kumbakonam)

Located in Darasuram near Kumbakonam, Tamil Nadu, the Airavatesvara Temple is a UNESCO World Heritage Site. This Hindu temple was built in the 12th century by Rajaraja Chola II of the Chola dynasty.

Dedicated to Lord Shiva, the temple is named after the white elephant, Airavata, who is believed to have worshipped Lord Shiva here. Therefore, Lord Shiva is worshipped here as Airavatesvara, or the deity of Airavata.

Everything in this temple is so mesmerizing that understanding it requires both time and insight. The carvings on the stones are other worldly. It is believed that the temple was constructed for entertainment purposes.

The temple's pillars rise 80 feet high. The southern part of the front mandapam is designed as a large chariot with stone wheels, being drawn by horses. To the east of the courtyard, there is a cluster of intricately carved buildings, one of which is known as Bali Peetam, or the place of sacrifice.

> On the seat of the Bali Peetam, there is a small temple with an image of Lord Ganesha. To the south of this seat, there is a set of three steps with exquisite carvings. These are the steps that, when lightly tapped with the feet, produce musical sounds.

Matangeshwar Mahadev Temple - Madhya Pradesh (Khajuraho)

Kedareshwar Cave Temple - Maharashtra (Ahmednagar)

In the southwest corner of the temple courtyard, there is a mandapam with four tirthas (holy places), one of which features an image of Yama, the god of death.

# The Temple with 33,000 Statues

## Meenakshi Amman Temple – Tamil Nadu (Madurai)

The Meenakshi Amman Temple is located in the city of Madurai, Tamil Nadu. The original name of Madurai is Madhurapuri (City of Sweetness), as it is believed that Goddess Parvati incarnated here as Meenakshi. The name 'Madurai' is a Tamil abbreviation for Madhurapuri (City of Sweetness). Goddess Parvati incarnated as the daughter of the King Malayadhwaja of Madurai. Lord Shiva, in the form of Sundareswarar, came and married Goddess Meenakshi. This temple is associated with many mythical stories and mysteries. One of the temple's mysteries is the statue of Meenakshi with three breasts. According to myths, Meenakshi was born with three breasts, and this extraordinary incarnation has its own mystery.

The Meenakshi Amman Temple is considered one of the most important temples in India. It was even included in the list of the Seven Wonders of the World. Meenakshi is considered an incarnation of Goddess Parvati.

Historians believe that this temple is over 2,500 years old. The sanctum sanctorum of the temple is 3,500 years old. The outer walls and the surrounding temple complex are over 1,500 to 2,000 years old. This grand temple is spread across 45 acres of land.

Both Lord Shiva (Sundareswarar) and Goddess Meenakshi are present in this temple. The temple has 12 grand gopurams (gateway towers), all beautifully sculpted. The temple also features 8 pillars, each with a statue of Goddess Lakshmi, and the pillars have inscriptions depicting the legendary stories of Lord Shiva. A finely carved statue of Lord Ganesha is also found in the temple.

> The unique feature of the Meenakshi Temple is that it houses two temples within its premises. One is the Meenakshi Temple, and the other is the Sundareswarar Temple. In the Meenakshi temple, one of her hands holds a parrot and the other a small sword. A depiction of a marriage celebration is engraved on the walls of this temple. In the Sundareswarar Temple, Lord Shiva, in his Sundareswarar form, is worshipped, and the marriage ceremony takes place. It is believed that every night, Lord Sundareswarar travels to the sanctum of Goddess Meenakshi, and the couple stays together without any disturbance. Besides the grand architecture, the statue of Goddess Meenakshi, with three breasts, remains a mystery for many.

# " The Temple Where Bricks Float, and Music Comes from Pillars "

## Ramappa Temple – Telangana (Mulugu)

In most cases, the names of temples are derived from the deities enshrined there. However, in India, there is one temple named after the person who constructed it, rather than the deity. This unique temple is known as the Ramappa Temple, located in the village of Palampet in the Mulugu district of Telangana.

> The biggest question that arises is: Where did such lightweight stones come from, as no such stones are found anywhere in the world that can float in water (except for the stones of Ram Setu)? Did Ramappa himself create such stones 800 years ago? Was there some kind of technology available to him that made the stones so light that they could float in water? The mystery of these stones remains unsolved even today.
>
> These stones are incredibly light, and when placed in water, they float rather than sink. This revelation helped uncover the secret behind the temple's durability: unlike other ancient temples that have collapsed under the weight of heavy stones, the Ramappa Temple was built using exceptionally light stones, which is why it has not crumbled.
>
> Even today, the temple stands as sturdy as it did in the past. A few years ago, when people raised the question of how the temple had withstood the test of time, the archaeology department visited Palampet to investigate. However, despite many

efforts, the mystery behind the temple's remarkable endurance was not unraveled.

The Ramappa Temple, dedicated to Lord Shiva, is also known as the Ramalingeswara Temple.

# The Temple Where Shadows Appear, but Not What They Seem

## Chaya Someswara Swamy Temple – Telangana (Nalgonda)

Many people were surprised to learn about the Chaya Someswara Swamy Temple, which has an ancient history associated with the Ikshvaku dynasty (lineage of Sri Rama).

Located on the outskirts of Panagal village in Nalgonda district, Telangana, this temple was constructed during the 11th and 12th centuries. The temple is known for its 'shadow' mystery, and the name "Chaya" (meaning shadow) was given due to a particular pillar in the temple.

> It is widely believed that a permanent shadow falls on the Shiva Lingam in the main temple throughout the day. The temple is a symbol of beauty, art, and magnificence, and it was engineered by the Kunduru Cholas and is accepted as a Trikutalayam. This is a testament to the creative vision and skill of its architects.
>
> In one of the sanctum sanctorums, on the western and eastern sides, there is always a shadow visible, and this mystery continues to attract thousands of visitors every year.

# An Unconquered Mountain Peak that No One has Climbed Yet

## Mount Kailash – Tibet (Mansarovar)

Mount Kailash is considered the center of the Earth, with heaven above it and the mortal world below. This place is filled with numerous mysteries. On one side of Kailash is the North Pole, and on the other side is the South Pole, with the Himalayas situated in between. Therefore, Kailash is regarded as the center of the Earth. According to scientists, this is also the center of the Earth. Mount Kailash is a significant spiritual hub for four major religions of the world: Hinduism, Jainism, Buddhism, and Sikhism.

> Mount Kailash is believed to be a center of supernatural powers where all ten directions meet, a concept referred to in scientific terms as "Axis Mundi." Axis Mundi means the navel of the world or the celestial pole, which is also called the geographic pole.
>
> Axis Mundi is a point that establishes a connection between the Earth and the sky, where all directions converge. According to Russian scientists, Axis Mundi is a place where supernatural or extraordinary power flows, and one can establish contact with these powers. Mount Kailash is the center of such powers.
>
> Mount Kailash resembles a giant pyramid, which is a center of 100 smaller pyramids. The structure of Kailash aligns with the four cardinal points on a compass and is located in such a secluded spot where no other major mountain exists.

Mount Kailash is an unconquered peak, as no one has climbed it yet. Consequently, climbing Mount Kailash has been prohibited. However, it is said that a Tibetan Buddhist monk, Milarepa, ascended it in the 11th century.

**There are two main lakes near this place –** The first is Mansarovar, the highest freshwater lake globally, shaped like the sun. The second is Rakshas Tal, the highest saltwater lake in the world, shaped like the moon.

These two lakes represent the forces of the sun and the moon, associated with positive and negative energy. When viewed from the south, they appear as a Swastika symbol. It remains a mystery whether these lakes formed naturally or were created.

From the four directions of Mount Kailash originate four rivers: the Brahmaputra, the Indus, the Sutlej, and the Karnali. These rivers give rise to other rivers like the Ganges, Saraswati, and various rivers in China. In each direction of Kailash, animal faces are seen, from which these rivers originate. In the east is the face of a horse, in the west an elephant, in the north a lion, and in the south a peacock.

Only virtuous souls can dwell in this area. Russian scientists studying Mount Kailash and its surroundings learned from spiritual leaders in Tibetan temples that an extraordinary energy field flows around Mount Kailash, where ascetics still maintain telepathic contact with spiritual masters.

A continuous sound is heard around the Kailash and Mansarovar Lake area, similar to the sound of an airplane flying nearby. But if one listens closely, the sound resembles that of a 'damaru' or 'Om.' Scientists suggest this could be due to the melting ice or the interaction of light and sound at this location, producing the sound of 'Om.'

It is claimed that seven types of lights can be seen shining in the sky over Mount Kailash. NASA scientists believe that this phenomenon could be due to the strong magnetic forces present here, which might create such lights when interacting with the atmosphere.

# Angkor Wat of Northeast India

## Unakoti Hill Temple - Tripura (Agartala)

Nestled in the forests of Tripura, Unakoti is a pilgrimage site primarily dedicated to Lord Shiva, believed to date back to the 7th - 9th century CE.

This temple is located about 125 kilometers from Tripura's capital, Agartala. It is considered one of the biggest mysteries of Northeast India. Surrounded by sprawling forests, narrow paths, and the sounds of gushing streams, lies the fascinating site of 'Unakoti' in Tripura.

This site remained largely unknown for many years, and even now, many people are unaware of its existence. The temple is as marvelous as it is captivating.

> There are a total of 99,99,999 stone sculptures here, whose mysteries remain unsolved till this day. Questions like who created these sculptures, when they were made, and why they were made remain unanswered. The most intriguing question is why there is one sculpture less than a crore. Various fascinating legends surround these sculptures.
>
> Due to these enigmatic sculptures, the site is named Unakoti, which means "one less than a crore." Two types of sculptures are found here – some are carved out of stones, while others are etched onto stone surfaces.

Most of the statues here are associated with Hindu deities, including Lord Shiva, Goddess Durga, Lord Vishnu, and Lord Ganesha.

At the center of this site is a gigantic statue of Lord Shiva, known as Unakotishwara. This statue of Lord Shiva stands approximately 30 feet tall.

In addition to the colossal statue of Lord Shiva, there are two other statues, including one of Goddess Durga. There are also three statues of Nandi here. Besides these, numerous other sculptures are scattered around the site.

One of the main attractions of this place is the extraordinary statues of Lord Ganesha. The statues depict Ganesha with four arms and three protruding tusks, a rare representation of the deity.

There are also two other statues of Ganesha with four tusks and eight arms. These unique statues make Unakoti a highly thrilling and fascinating destination.

# The Only Vishwanath Temple in the World Where Shiva Resides with Shakti

## Kashi Vishwanath Temple – Uttar Pradesh (Varanasi)

The city of Shiva, Kashi, is mentioned in several Puranas and scriptures. It is here in Kashi that one of the twelve famous Jyotirlingas of Lord Shiva, the Kashi Vishwanath Jyotirlinga, is located. At Kashi Vishwanath, Baba Bholenath resides in the form of Shakti with Goddess Bhagwati on his left.

The Jyotirlinga located in the present-day Varanasi holds immense significance in Hinduism. According to ancient beliefs, the Kashi Vishwanath Temple has existed in Varanasi for many thousands of years. It is religiously believed that a single visit to this temple and a holy dip in the Ganges can grant salvation.

> A legendary belief holds that the city of Varanasi is situated on the trident of Lord Shiva. It is also believed that when the Earth was created, the first ray of the sun fell on Kashi.
>
> The Kashi Vishwanath Jyotirlinga is constructed in two parts. On the right side of the Jyotirlinga, Goddess Bhagwati is seated as Shakti, while on the left side, Lord Shiva resides in his charming form. Since Goddess Bhagwati is seated on the right side here, the path to liberation is believed to open only in Kashi.

> At the Kashi Vishwanath Jyotirlinga, both Lord Shiva and Goddess Shakti are present together. There is no other place in the world where Lord Shiva and Goddess Shakti reside together, and the temple also has a Tantra entrance.

In Kashi, Baba Vishwanath is revered both as a guru and a king. Throughout the day, Baba roams Kashi in his guru form. When the nightly adornment and aarti of Baba Vishwanath take place at 9 PM, he is dressed as a king. Hence, Lord Shiva is also called Rajrajeshwar.

The Kashi Vishwanath Temple is also known as the Golden Temple. The dome of the Kashi Vishwanath Temple is made of gold. Maharaja Ranjit Singh of Punjab donated gold for this purpose.

Inside the sanctum sanctorum of the Kashi Vishwanath Temple, there is a mandap and a Shivling installed on a square silver platform. According to religious beliefs, a person who dies an untimely death cannot attain liberation without worshiping Shiva, but merely coming to Kashi grants them liberation.

The Jyotirlinga of Baba Vishwanath is located in the northeast corner of the sanctum sanctorum. The northeast corner signifies that this court of Baba is complete with all knowledge and arts.

Within the temple complex, there are also temples of Kalbhairav, Lord Vishnu, and Virupaksha Gauri. The Kashi Vishwanath Temple stands 15.5 meters tall. From the Tantra perspective, Baba Vishwanath's court has four major entrances: the Peace Gate, the Art Gate, the Prestige Gate, and the Liberation Gate.

# Where the Temple Doors Close as soon as the Sunsets

## Nidhivan Temple – Uttar Pradesh (Vrindavan)

Nidhivan (Tulsi Forest) is one of the sacred places in Vrindavan, located in the Mathura district of Uttar Pradesh, India. It is considered as a major site dedicated to the divine plays of the Hindu deities Radha and Krishna and their companions, the Gopis.

Among the devotees, there is a common belief that even today, Radha and Krishna perform their divine dance (Raas Leela) at night in Nidhivan. Hence, no one is allowed to stay inside the Nidhivan premises after nightfall. The courtyard is primarily filled with small and paired Tulsi (basil) plants. Apart from the Tulsi plants, the premises also house a temple of Lord Krishna known as 'Rang Mahal,' [*See* **Chapter 77** Temple where footprints of God are found] where it is believed that Radha and Krishna spend their night after the Raas Leela. Another temple within the premises is the 'Bansichor Radha Temple,' where it is said that Radha stole Krishna's flute.

Additionally, there is a shrine dedicated to Swami Haridas, who, with utmost devotion, crafted the idol of Banke Bihari. The complex also contains the 'Raas Leela Sthali' (the place where Raas Leela is performed) and the Lalita Kund. It is believed that when the Gopis asked for water during the Raas Leela, Krishna himself created the kund (pond).

The famous Vrindavan temple, known for its exquisite craftsmanship, is believed to host Shri Krishna and the Gopis at night for Raas Leela. Therefore, after the evening prayer, no one is seen in the temple. Even the animals and birds that roam around during the day leave the place after evening.

Let's explore more such intriguing and mysterious aspects of Nidhivan.

It is believed that Shri Krishna and Radha visit the Rang Mahal inside the Nidhivan every night. The temple is beautifully decorated for them, and when the temple is opened the next morning, it is found to be completely disheveled.

Devotees only offer items for adornment in the Rang Mahal, and in return, they receive similar items as prasad (offerings). Though the temple is closed after the evening, it is said that if anyone secretly watches the Raas Leela, they go mad the next day.

The trees growing in this temple complex also have a unique growth pattern. Generally, tree branches grow upwards, but here, they grow downward.

> Every Tulsi plant here is found in pairs. It is believed that during the night, these Tulsi plants transform into Gopis when Krishna and Radha perform Raas Leela and return to their original state by morning.
>
> It is also believed that no one can take even a single leaf from these Tulsi plants. It is said that anyone who has taken these leaves has faced calamities. Therefore, no one dares to touch them.
>
> The houses around Nidhivan do not have windows, and those that do, are closed after the sound of the evening prayer bell. It is believed that no one should look in this direction after 7 PM; if they do, they either go blind or face some severe misfortune.

Shri Krishna was always engrossed in playing his flute, so Radha stole it from him. In this temple, along with the idol of Radha, there is also an idol of Lalita, Krishna's most beloved Gopi.

Another temple within Nidhivan is the Vishakha Kund. It is believed that when Krishna was performing Raas Leela with the Gopis, one of his companions, Vishakha, felt thirsty. Seeing no water source, Krishna began digging with his flute, and the water that emerged quenched Vishakha's thirst. Since then, this pond has been known as Vishakha Kund.

# The Temple that Predicts the Monsoon Every Year

## Varsha Temple (Jagannath Temple) – Uttar Pradesh (Kanpur)

In the heart of Uttar Pradesh, approximately 125 km away, a three-and-a-half-hour drive from Lucknow and just 36 km, a one-and-a-half-hour drive from Kanpur, lies the tranquil village of Behta Buzurg, home to a mysterious temple — the Jagannath Temple. Its distinctive dome reflects the architectural beauty of West Bengal and Odisha.

This temple is full of contrasts, from its design to its main deity and its history. Over time, the temple has become more renowned due to the common belief among locals and worshippers that it accurately predicts the monsoon season every year.

> A week before the rain, the stone plate on the ceiling of the temple's innermost chamber becomes wet. If it remains dry, it indicates light rainfall for the year. However, if water droplets form on the ceiling, it signifies a good monsoon season ahead. For local farmers, this phenomenon acts as a divine prophecy, guiding their crucial decisions regarding the sowing of Kharif crops.
>
> Fifteen days before the rainfall, droplets start dripping from the temple's ceiling, signaling to the locals that rain will follow in 10 to 15 days. If the drips are sparse, it indicates very little rain. Conversely, if the droplets are heavy and persistent, it foretells heavy rainfall.

This temple is believed to be 5,000 years old. Inside, the idols of Lord Jagannath, Balabhadra (Baldev), and their sister Subhadra are enshrined. Additionally, the temple also houses the idol of Padmanabham.

# The Leaning Temple

## Ratneshwar Mahadev Temple – Uttar Pradesh (Varanasi)

Ratneshwar Mahadev Temple (also known as Matru-Rin Mahadev or the Leaning Temple of Varanasi) is located in the sacred city of Varanasi, Uttar Pradesh, India.

This temple was built very close to the Ganges River and has developed a tilt of nine degrees. In comparison, the Leaning Tower of Pisa in Italy leans at only four degrees. No one knows why the temple has developed such a significant tilt.

As with many structures and monuments in India, the legends and history surrounding the Ratneshwar Mahadev Temple do not align. The tilt could be the result of a structural issue, the fact that it was built on silt, or perhaps due to a curse.

No one knows why the temple was constructed so close to the riverbank. In fact, the temple is so close to the Ganges that part of it remains submerged throughout the year.

In the 19th century, when the temple's entrance would get submerged, priests would dive into the water to perform worship. Also known as Kashi Karvat (with Kashi being the ancient name for Varanasi and Karvat meaning tilted in Hindi), this temple was possibly built in the mid-19th century, either by a queen from Gwalior or the royal family of Amethi. Photographs of the temple from the 1860s show that it was not leaning at that time.

This amazing temple in Varanasi has been tilted at nine degrees for nearly 400 years. The Ratneshwar Temple stands 74 meters tall, which is about 20 meters taller than Italy's Leaning Tower of Pisa.

Described by locals and tourists as one of the world's most unique cities, 'Varanasi' aka 'Banaras' or 'Kashi' in Uttar Pradesh is a mesmerizing hub of tranquility. This ancient city has enough temples that accurately exemplify India's religious and spiritual culture. However, there is no temple quite like the Ratneshwar Mahadev Temple near Manikarnika Ghat. Dedicated to Lord Shiva, the Ratneshwar Temple is also known as the Matru-Rin Mahadev Temple or Kashi Karvat, meaning a tilted temple in Kashi.

The temple was constructed in the mid-19th century. Some photographs from the 1860s reveal the temple's mythical and religious significance. The temple's spire was built in the Nagara style of architecture with a pavilion adorned with pillars.

The temple is located in a very unusual place. Unlike other temples along the Ganges River in Varanasi, this temple is built at a much lower level, allowing the water level to reach the spire during the monsoon. The sanctum of the temple remains underwater for most of the year.

Everything about the Ratneshwar Temple is a puzzle, filled with numerous theories and myths.

> An 1882 photograph shows the Ratneshwar Mahadev Temple standing straight.
>
> In old photographs, the temple can be seen standing upright. However, in modern pictures, it appears tilted. According to information, at some point, the ghat collapsed and leaned, causing the temple to tilt. Except for those interested in spiritual sites, many travelers are still unaware of the temple.

# Birthplace of Lord Kalki Avatar

## Kalki Avatar Temple, Sambhal – Uttar Pradesh (Sambhal)

Sambhal is a town in the Sambhal district of the Indian state of Uttar Pradesh. It falls under the Sambhal Lok Sabha constituency.

### Religious Significance

In Satya Yuga, this place was known as Satyavrat, in Treta Yuga as Mahadgiri, in Dwapara Yuga as Pingal, and in Kali Yuga, it is known as Sambhal. It houses 68 pilgrimages and 19 wells. There is an ancient, grand temple here, along with three main Shivlingas: Chandrashekhar in the east, Bhubaneswar in the north, and Sambhaleshwar in the south. Every year on Kartik Shukla Chaturthi and Panchami, a fair is held, and pilgrims circumambulate the area. Sambhal is also a commercial center for agricultural products. The ancient place mentioned by Ptolemy as Sambalk is equated with Sambhal. It is a common belief that in the Kali Yuga, the Kalki Avatar will take place in a village called Shambhal. Popular belief equates Sambhal with Shambhal. This place, known for its handcrafted products at the national and international levels, is famous because of its many historical sites.

According to Puranas, it is believed that Lord Vishnu's tenth incarnation, Shri Kalki Bhagwan, will be born in Sambhal in Kali Yuga. This belief led to the establishment of a temple here about 1,000 years ago. The temple's Mahant claims that this is the only temple of Kalki Bhagwan in the country.

As per the **Kalki Purana**, Lord Kalki will ride a horse named Devadatta, which will be white, and his weapon will be a bow and arrow. Kalki, the tenth incarnation of Vishnu, will possess 64 arts. His guru will be Parashurama, who will guide Kalki to perform penance to Lord Shiva and gain divine powers. It is believed that the Kalki Avatar will mark the end of Kali Yuga. According to **Kalki Purana**, Lord

Vishnu will incarnate to destroy evil and resurrect Satya Yuga. The Kalki Avatar will protect the righteous and annihilate sinners.

## History

Sambhal has been a significant settlement since ancient times, even during Muslim rule. In the late 15th and early 16th centuries, it was one of the provincial capitals under Sikandar Lodi. This ancient city was once the capital of the great Chauhan emperor Prithviraj Chauhan, and it is believed to be the place where he was killed by Afghans in the second battle. Sambhal is also known for the phrase "Makaan Toote Log Jhoote" (Houses crumble, people lie), although this has no basis in reality. Some residents still claim its truth. In the 1991 census, Sambhal was found to have the lowest literacy rate in the country, but conditions have improved over time.

During the medieval period, Sambhal gained strategic importance due to its proximity to Agra and Delhi. During Babur's invasion, Sambhal's territory was under the control of Afghan chieftains. Babur assigned the Sambhal estate to Humayun, who fell ill and was brought to Agra. After Babur, Humayun divided the empire among his brothers, and Sambhal was given to Askari. Sher Shah Suri expelled Humayun and assigned the estate of Sambhal to his son-in-law Mubarez Khan. According to Abbas Khan Sherwani, Babur's commanders demolished several temples and Jain statues in the area.

# Upon Entering the Temple, the Biggest Liars Speak the Truth

## Narsingh Baba's Temple – Uttar Pradesh (Mau)

In this miraculous temple, even the biggest liars start speaking the truth as soon as they step inside, a miracle that has been happening for years.

This temple is the Narsingh Baba's temple, located in the Dagoli Gram Sabha of Mau district in Uttar Pradesh. The temple houses the shrine of Narsingh Baba and nearby is a temple dedicated to Lord Hanuman.

The priest of this temple, Mahant, states that this temple is indeed very miraculous. If people sincerely make a vow here, their wishes are fulfilled. If someone is suspected of lying, they are brought to this temple, made to stand on a wooden platform under a Peepal tree, and made to swear.

> **A Mysterious Temple in UP**
>
> The person who lies starts speaking the truth on their own. If anyone lies, something unfortunate happens to them, be it an illness or a family accident. This is why people are afraid to take false oaths here.
>
> Those who take false oaths never come near this temple, because as soon as they approach, they start confessing the truth. This is why no one dares to take a false oath here. The specialty of

this temple is that if someone wearing yellow clothes takes a false oath while standing on a wooden platform under the Peepal tree, the truth emerges from their mouth, and they become restless.

**Every Wish is Fulfilled Here!**

It is said that there was an ascetic named Narsingh Baba who meditated and took Samadhi in this temple. Following this, the temple was constructed in his honour, and a statue of Lord Hanuman was also installed beside it. Visitors first worship at the shrine of Narsingh Baba before proceeding to Lord Hanuman. It is believed that if one makes a wish here with a sincere heart, it is granted.

# Temple Where the Sound of Water Comes from the Steps

## Ganga Temple – Uttar Pradesh (Hapur)

Crowds gather to visit the ancient Ganga Temple in Garhmukteshwar. This temple is situated on an 80-foot-high mound. It is believed that wishes made here are fulfilled, and devotees offer offerings upon their wishes being granted. A unique feature of the temple is that when a stone is thrown on the temple's steps, it produces a sound similar to that of a stone hitting water. It seems as if the Ganges flows by touching the temple steps.

The ancient and historical Ganga Temple, located on the edge of the city of Garh Ganga, stands atop an approximately 80-foot-high mound. There used to be 101 steps leading to this temple, but due to road elevation over time, only 84 steps remain. The temple houses a life-sized statue of Goddess Ganga, a four-faced statue of Lord Brahma in milk-white colour, and a Shivling.

### Special Stone on the Temple Steps

A special type of stone is installed on the temple steps. When a stone is thrown from above onto these steps, it produces a sound similar to a stone hitting water. Every year, a Shiv figure naturally emerges on the temple's Shivling.

Scientists have not yet been able to uncover why this happens. The temple also features a four-faced white statue of Lord Brahma. The origin and founder of the temple remain unknown.

## 101 Steps Built with the Help of the Administration

According to ancestors, the temple's history is thousands of years old. Initially, there were no steps or boundary walls around the temple. The Ganges used to flow through this temple, but now it has shifted about five kilometers away to the Amroha district. Previously, the district administration was responsible for maintaining the temples, and a portion of the income from the Ganga Bath Fair was spent on the upkeep of the temples. Between 1885 and 1890, with the administration's assistance, 101 steps were constructed to reach the temple.

# Temple Where Footprints of God are Found

## Rangmahal Temple – Uttar Pradesh (Mathura)

India is home to many unique and astonishing temples, one of which is the temple of Lord Krishna in Vrindavan. This temple, located in Nidhivan, is exceptionally unique. It opens and closes by itself, and is known as Rangmahal. The priests believe that Lord Krishna comes here every night to sleep.

### Bed Arranged for Lord Krishna's Sleep

A bed is meticulously prepared for Lord Krishna's sleep in the temple, complete with clean mattresses and sheets. When the temple opens, the creases in the bedding indicate that someone has indeed slept there. Another mysterious occurrence in this temple is that every day, butter and sugar candy are offered as prasad. Whatever remains is left in the temple, but by morning, it is gone, believed to have been consumed by Lord Krishna.

Saint Haridas, the guru of Tansen, is said to have invoked the divine presence of Radha and Krishna through his hymns in this temple. Krishna and Radha are believed to come here to perform Raas Leela. There is also a shrine dedicated to Swamiji here. It is said that if anyone secretly watches the Raas Leela at night, they either lose their eyesight or go mad. Hence, no windows are installed in the nearby houses, and people do not enter the temple premises after the evening aarti. The temple complex has two Tulsi plants, believed to transform into Krishna's Gopis at night and dance with him.

[*See* also **Chapter 71** where the Temple Doors close as soon as the sunsets]

# Temple that Opens Only Once a Year

## Latu Devta Temple – Uttarakhand (Chamoli)

In the village of Wan, located in Chamoli district of Uttarakhand, there exists a unique temple called the *Latu Devta Temple*. This temple is frequently discussed among the locals due to several intriguing facts associated with it, which are sure to astonish anyone who learns about them. The most remarkable aspect of this temple is that the priests perform rituals with blindfolds on their eyes and cloths covering their mouths. Additionally, the temple holds immense significance among the people, but regular visitors are not allowed to enter and view the idol inside.

> In the village of Wan, Chamoli district, there is a temple that opens only once a year. Despite this, people, due to fear, visit the temple only from the outside to pay their respects. It is said that inside the temple, the serpent king (Nagraj) resides with his precious gem (Mani). The glow of this gem is so intense that it can cause blindness, and people can go blind if exposed to its light. This is the reason why no devotee dares to enter the temple. Only the priest is allowed to go inside, and even they cover their eyes, nose, and mouth with cloth, as they believe the air inside may contain poisonous fumes from the serpent king, and the poison should not enter their body through their nose or mouth. Hence, they cover their face with cloth.
>
> This is why ordinary people cannot enter the temple to have darshan (viewing of the idol).

This temple is called *Latu Devta Temple*, and darshan (viewing) of it is considered very rare. Latu Devta is said to be seated in the form of a snake inside the temple, and worship is conducted on the full moon day of the month of Vaishakh.

> The doors of the Latu Devta Temple open only once a year, on the full moon day of the Vaishakh month. On this day, a crowd of devotees gathers to seek darshan. The doors are then closed on the new moon day of the month of Margashirsha.

# Lake of Skeletons

## Roopkund Lake - Uttarakhand (Chamoli)

Our country is home to many beautiful places that are admired by the world. However, some mysterious locations exist that send chills down people's spines once their secrets are revealed.

One such place is Roopkund Lake, also known as the *Lake of Skeletons*. In this lake, many human skeletons can still be found floating. Located in the Chamoli district of Uttarakhand, Roopkund Lake is famous among trekkers. People from far and wide visit this mysterious lake to witness its eerie presence.

In 1942, British forest guards discovered hundreds of human skeletons floating in the water at this lake. At that time, the entire lake was filled with human skeletons and bones. The discovery of such a large number of bones and human skeletons led people to speculate various theories.

Initially, people assumed that these skeletons might belong to Japanese soldiers who, during World War II, had tried to invade India through the Himalayan route and had died in the snowy cliffs.

The British government called in a team of scientists to study these human remains. The investigation revealed that these skeletons did not belong to Japanese soldiers; rather, they were much older. These skeletons were subjected to periodic tests. Some scientists believed that these people had perished in a disaster caused by an avalanche many years ago, while others suggested that they had died due to an epidemic.

To date, between 600-800 human skeletons have been found in the lake. Some of the skeletons still have remnants of flesh. DNA tests on these skeletons revealed traces of various geographical regions. Finally, the scientists concluded that these people had died a long time ago due to heavy round objects falling on their heads. In conclusion, all the scientists agreed that these individuals had perished during a heavy hailstorm.

# The Temple that Remained intact depite being Buried in Snow for 400 Years and was Miraculously Protected by a huge rock from Devastating Floodwaters

## Shri Kedarnath Dham Temple – Uttarakhand (Rudraprayag)

The Kedarnath Dham is held in deep reverence by devotees, and at the same time, it has sparked much curiosity. There are many mysteries associated with the Kedarnath Dham and temple, and if one tries to solve them using the logic of science, they only seem to become more perplexing.

After Adi Shankaracharya, the temple was renovated time and again. It is said that the temple was first renovated in the 10th century by King Bhoj of Malwa and again in the 13th century. The gates of the Kedarnath temple open in the month of May and are closed during the winter after the festival of Diwali and the occasion of Bhai Dooj.

Located on the Kedarnath peak of the Gariraj Himalayas in Uttarakhand, this temple is one of the twelve Jyotirlingas of India. The Kedarnath Dham is surrounded by mysteries, with many legends connected to it.

For 400 years, the Kedarnath temple remained buried under snow, and when it emerged from the snow, it was found to be completely intact. According to Vijay Joshi, a scientist from the Wadia Institute of Himalayan Geology in Dehradun, a small ice age occurred between the 13th and 17th centuries, during which a large part of the Himalayas, including this temple region, was covered by snow. Scientists believe that signs of this can still be seen on the temple walls and stones.

Kedarnath is part of the Chorabari Glacier. Scientists say that due to the continuous melting of glaciers and the shifting of rocks, such natural calamities may continue in the future.

The Kedarnath peak is situated at an altitude of around 22,000 feet, while the other nearby peaks–Chorakund and Bhartkund–are at 21,600 feet and 22,700 feet respectively. Additionally, the confluence of five rivers–Mandakini, Madhuganga, Ksheerganga, Saraswati, and Swarnagauri–can be found here. The Mandakini River, a tributary of the Alaknanda, still flows here, and Kedarnath is situated on its banks. The area is known for heavy snow and rainfall during winters.

The temple is constructed using large, sturdy brown-coloured stones known as *Katwan Patthar*. It stands on a six-foot-high platform, with the temple itself being 85 feet tall, 187 feet long, and 80 feet wide. The walls of the temple are 12 feet thick. It is a wonder how such heavy stones were transported to this height and shaped to form a temple, especially the massive roof, which rests on columns. The interlocking technique was used to join the stones together.

The temple was first constructed by the Pandavas, but it was lost over time due to the ravages of time. The present temple was built by Adi Shankaracharya, who was born in 508 BCE and passed away in 476 BCE. His samadhi lies behind the temple. The inner sanctum of the temple is believed to be quite ancient, dating back to the 8th century. The temple was renovated again in the 10th century by King Bhoj of Malwa and later in the 13th century.

After the grand festival of Diwali, during the winter season, the doors of the temple are closed. For six months, a lamp remains lit inside the temple. The priests respectfully close the doors, taking the deity's idol and staff to Ukhimath, located at a lower altitude, for the winter. After six months, the temple doors are reopened in May, marking the beginning of the pilgrimage season in Uttarakhand. During these six months, no one stays near the temple. It is amazing that even during this period, the lamp

Kailash Temple - Maharashtra (Aurangabad)

Shree Jagannath Temple - Odisha (Puri)

continues to burn, and the rituals continue. Upon reopening, the temple is found to be in the exact same condition, as if no time has passed.

On the night of June 16, 2013, nature unleashed its fury. A devastating flood caused large, strong buildings to collapse like a house of cards and wash away. However, the Kedarnath temple remained untouched. What was even more miraculous was that a massive rock, rolling down from the mountainside, suddenly stopped right behind the temple! This rock obstructed the floodwaters, dividing them into two parts, and the temple became even more secure. Around 10,000 people lost their lives in this disaster.

According to the prophecies of the Puranas, the entire area of Kedarnath and Badrinath is predicted to vanish. It is believed that when the Nar and Narayan peaks merge, the route to Badrinath will be completely closed, and devotees will no longer be able to visit Badrinath. The Puranas predict that both the Kedarnath and Badrinath temples will be lost, and in the future, a new pilgrimage site called *Bhavishya Badri* will emerge.

# The Land of Apsaras

## Khait Parvat - Uttarakhand (Tehri)

Khait Parvat is situated at an altitude of approximately 10,000 feet above sea level. It is located about 5 kilometers from the Thaat village in the mysterious Ghanasali region. Khait Parvat is nothing less than a paradise. It is believed that people still experience sudden glimpses of apsaras (celestial nymphs) here. According to local belief, the apsaras of Khait Parvat protect the village.

In the local language, apsaras are referred to as *Aanchariyas*.

**Khait Parvat** is also considered mysterious because fruits and flowers bloom here throughout the year. However, when these fruits and flowers are moved from one place to another, they spoil instantly. Despite this, walnut and garlic crops thrive naturally on this desolate mountain. The walnut orchards are located near the Garbh Zone cave of the Maa Baradi temple on the Luki Pidi mountain.

**The Mysterious Khaitkhal Temple**

Located 5 kilometers from Thaat village in the Khait Parvat region, the Khaitkhal Temple is also known as a center of mysterious powers. Locals worship it as the temple of fairies or *Aanchariyas*. A fair is held here every year in the month of June. It is believed that the fairies dislike bright colors, noise, and loud music, which is why these are prohibited in the area.

There is also a well-known story in the region about a man named Jeetu. It is said that the fairies were drawn to Jeetu's flute playing, and they appeared before him and took him with them.

There is some force here that attracts people. It is believed that nine fairies reside on this mountain. The most astonishing thing is that the *Okhalis* (grain pounders), which are usually found on flat surfaces, are found built into the walls on Khait Parvat.

> **The Mysterious Temple, Where the Idol of the Goddess Changes Its Form Three Times a Day**

## Dhari Devi Temple – Uttarakhand (Srinagar)

> India has no shortage of mysterious and ancient temples. One such temple is located about 14 kilometers from Srinagar in Uttarakhand, where a miracle happens every day, leaving people astonished. In this temple, the idol of the goddess changes its form three times a day. In the morning, the idol appears as a young girl, then in the afternoon, it takes the form of a young woman, and in the evening, it transforms into an old woman. This sight is truly astonishing.

This temple is known as the Dhari Devi Temple. It is located in the middle of a lake. Dedicated to Goddess Kali, the temple is believed to protect the Char Dham of Uttarakhand. This goddess is regarded as the protector of the mountains and pilgrims.

According to a mythological story, the temple was once washed away in a severe flood. Along with it, the idol of the goddess was also carried away and stopped after hitting a rock near Dharo village. It is said that a divine voice emanated from the idol, instructing the villagers to install the idol at that spot. Subsequently, the villagers built a temple there. Priests believe that the idol of Goddess Dhari has been in the temple since the Dwapar Yuga.

It is said that the Dhari Devi Temple was demolished in 2013, and the idol was moved from its original location, which led to a devastating flood in Uttarakhand that year, claiming the lives of thousands of people. It is believed that the idol was removed from its original place on the evening of June 16, 2013, and a disaster struck the state just hours later. Later, the temple was rebuilt at the same location.

# The Mysterious Temple, Where Corpses Come to Life in Front of the Shiva Lingam

## Mahamundeshwar/Lakhamandal Shiva Temple – Uttarakhand (Dehradun)

About 128 kilometers from Dehradun, the capital of Uttarakhand, is an extraordinary Shiva temple. Located in Lakhamandal, it is also known as the Lakhamandal Shiva Temple. This temple is famous for its mysterious powers. It is believed that placing a corpse in front of the Shiva Lingam here brings it back to life for a short while. According to the myth, during the Mahabharata period, Duryodhan attempted to burn the Pandavas alive here. During their exile, Yudhishthir established the Shiva Lingam at this spot, which still stands in the temple today.

> The Shiva Lingam in this temple is known as Mahamundeshwar. It is believed that when a dead person is placed in front of the Shiva Lingam and sanctified water is sprinkled by the priest, the person comes to life for a brief moment. The revived person then chants Shiva's name, drinks the holy Ganga water, and their soul leaves the body again.

During the Mahabharata period, Duryodhan had built a Lakshagriha (house of lac) to burn the Pandavas. However, they escaped from a secret cave. Another belief is that Yudhishthir created the Shiva Lingam here, which is still present in the temple.

When a corpse is placed near the Shiva Lingam, it is revived for a short time. After being revived, the person drinks the holy Ganga water, and moments later, their soul departs from the body. Excavations in the area have unearthed various shapes and types of Shiva Lingams. The temple is located near the Yamuna River, in a place called Baranigarh.

Two doorkeepers stand as guards at the rear of the temple, one of whom has a severed hand, which remains an unsolved mystery. Also, the face of the person performing the ritual at the Shiva Lingam is clearly visible in the water.

It is believed that women who wish to conceive and sit in front of the temple on Maha Shivaratri night, staring at the temple's lamp and chanting Shiva mantras, will be blessed with a son within the year.

# The 1200-Year-Old Narsingh Dev Temple

## Narsingh Temple – Uttarakhand (Chamoli)

Joshimath is one of the sacred religious sites and is currently in the news due to continuous land sinking. Surrounded by the snow-covered Himalayan mountains, Joshimath is home to many major Hindu pilgrimage sites, including the Narsingh Temple. The idol of Lord Narsingh was installed here by Adi Shankaracharya, and one of its arms continues to become thinner.

In Joshimath, cracks have started appearing in the roads, homes, and temples, including the world-famous and religiously significant Narsingh Temple. The walls of the Narsingh Temple have developed cracks, and the idol of Lord Narsingh is in a calm posture, with one of its arms becoming thinner over time.

### The Connection Between the Narsingh Temple and Lord Badrinath

The Narsingh Temple in Joshimath sees a constant stream of visitors throughout the year, and it is believed to be nearly a thousand years old. During the winter season, Lord Badrinath resides at this temple, which is considered his winter seat. Here, worship is performed in honor of Lord Badrinath. It is believed that the pilgrimage to Badrinath is not complete without visiting the Narsingh Temple in Joshimath. Therefore, this temple is also known as Narsingh Badrinath.

## Beliefs Associated with the Narsingh Temple in Joshimath

There are various beliefs regarding this temple, but the *Rajatarangini* text mentions that this temple was built in the 8th century by the Kashmiri king Lalitaditya Muktapida. Another belief is that the Pandavas laid the foundation of this temple, and yet another belief is that Adi Guru Shankaracharya installed the idol of Lord Narsingh because he regarded him as his personal deity. The temple also houses the seat of Adi Guru Shankaracharya. Some people believe that the idol of Lord Narsingh appeared spontaneously.

## The Idol of Lord Narsingh is Made of Shaligrama Stone

The idol of Lord Narsingh in the Narsingh Badrinath Temple is about 10 inches tall and is made of Shaligrama stone. The idol is seated on a lotus. Besides Lord Narsingh, idols of Badrinarayana, Kubera, and Uddhava are also installed in the temple. On the right side of Lord Narsingh, there are idols of Ram, Sita, Hanuman, and Garuda, and on the left side, there is an idol of Kalika Mata.

### The Mystery of the Thinning Arm of Lord Narsingh

The right arm of the idol of Lord Narsingh in the temple is thin, and it continues to become thinner every year. The *Kedarkhand* text, in the *Sanat Kumar Samhita*, mentions that one day this arm will break off, and when that happens, the mountains named Nar and Narayan will merge, and pilgrims will no longer be able to visit Lord Badrinath. It is said that at that time, the *Bhavishya Badrinath* Temple in Joshimath will become the place for Badrinath's darshan.

### The Prophecy at Bhavishya Badrinath Temple in Joshimath

There is a stone near the Bhavishya Badrinath Temple, on which Adi Guru Shankaracharya wrote a prophecy. However, no one has been able to read this prophecy to date. Joshimath is also connected to the Ramayana and Mahabharata periods. It is believed that Lord Hanuman came here in search of the Sanjeevani herb, where he fought the demon Kalnemi, and the ground where Hanuman killed the demon still appears to be covered with red mud.

## The Story of the Thinning Arm of Narsingh

A popular story in Joshimath mentions a king named Vasudev who once ruled the area. One day, while he was out hunting in the forest, Lord Narsingh arrived at the king's palace and asked the queen for food. The queen respectfully served Lord Narsingh. After the meal, Lord Narsingh asked to rest on the king's bed. Meanwhile, the king returned from his hunt and entered his room.

The king saw a man lying on his bed and, in a fit of rage, struck him with his sword. Instead of blood, milk flowed from the man's wound, and the man transformed into Lord Narsingh. Realizing his mistake, the king sought forgiveness, and Lord Narsingh said that the punishment for his crime would be that he would leave Joshimath with his family and settle in Kartyur. Lord Narsingh also said that as a result of the king's blow, the arm of the idol in the temple would continue to thin, and one day, when it falls, the king's dynasty will end.

# A Temple Where Chinese Priests Offer Prayers to Kali Mata and Chinese Food is Prasad

## Chinese Kali Temple – West Bengal (Kolkata)

In Kolkata, there is a place called Tangra, also known as China Town, where many Chinese people have settled. In Tangra, there is a Kali Mata temple that appears like any other temple, but what makes it unique is that the offerings given in the temple are Chinese food such as momo, chowmein, and other Chinese dishes. It is believed that about 60 years ago, a Chinese boy fell seriously ill, and doctors could not cure him. In desperation, his parents brought him to this place, where two stones under a tree were worshiped as the form of Kali Mata. After performing the worship, the boy was miraculously cured, and his parents decided to build a temple at that location. Over time, both local people and Chinese people developed faith in Kali Mata, and they began visiting the temple.

Today, both Hindu and Chinese priests perform worship together at the temple, and Chinese incense is burned inside the temple.

# " Natural Cave Temples "

## Gupteshwar Mahadev (Guptadham Cave Temple) – Bihar (Rohtas)

Guptadham Cave Temple is located in the Chenari block of Rohtas district in Bihar. Situated in a cave on the Kaimur hills, the Guptadham houses the famous Gupteshwar Mahadev Temple, which is renowned as a Shaiva center. Lord Shiva is one of the three main deities in Hinduism, and the path to this sacred site is quite difficult. Just as people endure various hardships to reach the holy shrines of Kedarnath and Badrinath, similarly, devotees reach this unique shrine of Lord Shiva.

An adventurous and pleasant journey, where one encounters the ups and downs of the mountains, waterfalls, rivers, and forests. This journey is to Guptadhham in the Chenari block of Rohtas district in Bihar.

The cave in which Lord Shiva resides in this temple is of unknown age, and there is no concrete evidence regarding its age. However, based on its structure, it is believed that this cave was created by humans. According to tradition, performing a water ritual (Jalabhishek) in the temple's cave at Guptadhham fulfills all the wishes of the devotees.

Just as many people experience oxygen deficiency during the Kedarnath pilgrimage, similarly, visitors to this sacred place also face oxygen shortages. It is said that in 1989, nearly half a dozen people lost their lives due to lack of oxygen, but despite this, a large crowd of devotees continues to visit the place.

After reaching the entrance of this sacred cave located on the mountain, one has to descend the stairs. Near the entrance, there is an arch-shaped door that is 18 feet wide and 12 feet high. As you walk straight in the eastern direction, complete darkness envelops you. After moving about 363 feet inside the cave, there is a large pit that remains filled with water throughout the year, which is why it is called 'Patal Ganga.'

Beyond this point, the cave becomes quite narrow. Inside the cave, rare ancient rock paintings still exist. From the middle of this cave, another branch of the cave emerges, which forms a chamber ahead. This chamber is referred to as the "Naach Ghar" or "Ghuddaund" by the locals.

Due to the lack of proper lighting, devotees are unable to view the Naach Ghar. Moving west from here, another narrow branch goes rightward. The next section is called Tulsi Chawra.

From this junction, another cave extends a little further south and then turns west. In this cave is the Shivling known as Gupteshwar Mahadev. This Shivling is a natural formation within the cave. Water continuously drips from the ceiling of the cave onto the Shivling. Devotees take this water as prasad. About one and a half kilometers south of Guptadhham, there is Sita Kund, whose water remains consistently cold. Taking a bath here is a truly wonderful experience.

One mystery of this cave has never been solved. In fact, the source of the water that constantly drips onto the Shivling inside the cave remains unknown to this day.

Legend has it that once Bhasmasura was performing a penance to please Lord Shiva. Pleased with Bhasmasura's penance, Lord Shiva granted him a boon, asking him to wish for anything. Bhasmasura said that whoever's head he puts his hand on should be burnt to ashes. Lord Shiva granted him this boon.

Then, fascinated by the beauty of Goddess Parvati, Bhasmasura wanted to place his hand on Lord Shiva's head. To save himself from Bhasmasura, Lord Shiva had to hide in this cave. Seeing this, Lord

Vishnu took the form of Mohini and cleverly tricked Bhasmasura into placing his hand on his own head, thereby turning him into ashes.

In the historic Gupteshwar Mahadev, there is an old tradition of offering Ganga water from Buxar on the Shivling. Especially on the occasion of Shivratri, people from Jharkhand, Uttar Pradesh, Madhya Pradesh, Bihar, Chhattisgarh, and even Nepal come here to perform water offerings (Jalabhishek).

# In the Lap of the Mountains Resides Goddess Durga Herself

## Shri Mata Vaishno Devi Temple – Jammu and Kashmir (Katra)

The famous Hindu pilgrimage site, the Vaishno Devi Temple, is located in Jammu, Jammu and Kashmir, India. During the Navratri festival, a large number of pilgrims visit this temple. Above the Vaishno Devi Temple is a famous temple dedicated to Bhairon Baba. During winter, there is snowfall here, while in the summer, the temperature is suitable for tourists. Let's explore the mysteries of this temple.

Located at an elevation of approximately 5,200 feet on the Trikuta Hill, this temple is the second most visited religious site in India after the Tirumala Venkateswara Temple. The pilgrimage to Vaishno Devi begins from Katra, which is about 13 kilometers to the temple and about 14.5 kilometers to the Bhairon temple. In a cave on the Trikuta Hill, there are three self-manifested idols of Goddess Vaishno Devi: Goddess Kali (on the right), Goddess Saraswati (on the left), and Goddess Lakshmi (in the center), represented as Pindis. The combined form of these three Pindis is known as Vaishno Devi Mata. This place is referred to as Mata's Bhawan. The sacred cave is 98 feet long. In this cave, there is a large platform with Mata's seat where Devi Trikuta resides along with her divine forms.

The Bhawan is the place where Mata killed Bhairavnath. Before the ancient cave, Bhairav's body is present, and his head flew off and landed three kilometers away in the Bhairon Valley, while the body remained there. The spot where his head fell is now known as the 'Bhairav Nath Temple.'

Once, Bhairavnath chased a beautiful maiden on the Trikuta Hill. As he attempted to catch her, she transformed into wind and flew towards the Trikuta mountain. Bhairavnath pursued her, and it is believed that at that moment, Hanuman Ji arrived to protect the goddess. When Hanuman Ji became thirsty, Mata shot an arrow from her bow, causing a stream of water to flow from the mountain. She washed her hair in this water and then entered a cave, where she meditated for nine months, with Hanuman Ji guarding the entrance. During this time, a sage told Bhairavnath that the maiden he was chasing was none other than the Adishakti, Jagadamba, and he should stop pursuing her. Bhairavnath ignored the sage's advice, and Mata exited the cave through another opening. This cave is still known as Ardhkumari or Adikumari (the cave of the first manifestation) and before Ardhkumari, there is also Mata's charan paduka which is famous for being the place where Mata turned around and saw Bhairavnath.

Bhairavnath reached the cave entrance and tried to enter, but the maiden transformed into the form of Devi and ordered Bhairavnath to return. However, Bhairavnath didn't comply and attempted to enter. Seeing this, Hanuman Ji, who was guarding the cave, challenged Bhairavnath to battle. A fierce fight ensued, and as there was no conclusion to the fight, Mata Vaishno Devi assumed the form of Mahakali and killed Bhairavnath.

It is said that after his death, Bhairavnath repented for his actions and sought forgiveness from the Goddess. Mata Vaishno Devi knew that Bhairavnath's main intention behind attacking her was to attain liberation. Thus, she granted him release from the cycle of rebirth and blessed him, saying that her devotees' worship would not be complete until they visit Bhairavnath's temple after visiting hers.

Another miracle occurs in this sacred cave. Sacred Ganga water continually flows from it. This cave is also known as 'Garbha Gufa' (womb cave), as it is believed that Mata Vaishno stayed in this cave for nine months. Pilgrims are allowed to enter this cave only once; they cannot go in again. Those who do manage to stay in this Garbha Gufa are believed to live a life of peace and happiness.

> This Trikuta Mountain is mentioned in Rigveda. It is believed that the blessings of Goddess Parvati radiate upon

this cave, where 33 categories of gods (12 Adityas, 11 Rudras, 8 Vasus, and 2 Ashwini Kumaras) are always in devotion of the Goddess. The cave used to be quite narrow until 1977, when a new cave was constructed. Now, devotees enter through one cave and exit through another. It is said that only a fortunate few are able to experience the divine darshan of Mata Vaishno Devi. The body of Bhairavnath, whom Mata killed with a trident, is kept at the temple, and his head is said to have flown to Bhairav Valley. This remains the reason why his body remains there.

# A Unique Example of Sculpture and Painting Art

## Ajanta Caves – Maharashtra (Aurangabad)

The Ajanta Caves are a series of 29 Buddhist rock-cut cave monuments located in the state of Maharashtra, India, created between the 2nd century BCE and approximately 480 CE. Universally regarded as masterpieces of Buddhist religious art, the caves include paintings and rock-cut sculptures that are considered some of the finest surviving examples of ancient Indian art, particularly the expressive paintings that convey emotions through gestures, postures and forms.

More than 80% of the Ajanta Caves were vihars (temporary resting places for travelers, monasteries). The designers and artisans who created these caves also included provisions for collecting donations and storing grains and food for visitors and monks. Several caves contain large storage chambers carved into the floors. According to Spink, the largest storage areas are found in the temples of Ajanta Cave 6 and Cave 11, located in very spacious sections. These caves were possibly chosen for their relative convenience and the high level of security provided to those using them. The decision to integrate covered vaults carved into the floors could have been influenced by the need for easy access to space and supplies.

- ◆ The construction of the Ajanta Caves took place over a span of 800 years, from the 2nd century BCE to the 6th century CE. The Ellora Caves, on the other hand, were built between the 6th and 10th centuries. Both the Ajanta and Ellora caves are examples of ancient Indian rock-cut architecture. They are famous for their exceptional sculptures, paintings, and architectural designs.

- The Ajanta Caves are renowned for their unique paintings, which depict scenes from the life of Buddha as well as several other Buddhist deities and figures. The Ellora Caves are famous for their massive sculptures including the Kailash Temple, a huge temple dedicated to Lord Shiva, which was carved from a single piece of rock. The caves were constructed by carving rocks using simple tools like hammers and chisels. The process was slow and labor-intensive, and the resulting structures are considered marvels of ancient engineering.

- The Ajanta Caves were designed to capture natural light entering the cave, creating a dramatic and awe-inspiring effect. The caves were abandoned by the 10th century and, over time, became overgrown with vegetation and forgotten. They were rediscovered in 1819 by a group of British soldiers.

  - The identity of the artisans who carved the caves remains unknown.
  - It is unclear how these artisans were able to create such intricate designs and sculptures using only simple tools.
  - The meaning behind some of the paintings and sculptures remains a mystery, as much of the context surrounding their creation has been lost over time.
  - The use and abandonment of the caves for religious purposes remain shrouded in mystery.
  - Some experts believe there may be additional unknown caves in the surrounding area, yet to be discovered.

> **A Massive Temple Resting on a Single Pillar**

## Kedareshwar Cave Temple – Maharashtra (Ahmednagar)

This temple is located in the Harishchandragad hill of Ahmednagar district in Maharashtra and is dedicated to Lord Shiva. The temple is situated inside a cave, and in the center of the cave, there is a 5-foot high Shiva Lingam. Around this Lingam, there is water up to waist height, and devotees stand in the water to perform the worship of the Shiva Lingam. The most surprising aspect of this temple is the presence of four pillars inside the cave, three of which are broken, and only one remains intact. These four pillars are associated with the four ages (Satya Yuga, Treta Yuga, Dwapar Yuga, and Kali Yuga), and it is believed that whenever a pillar breaks, an age comes to an end. The last remaining pillar is associated with Kali Yuga, and it is believed that the day this pillar breaks, Kali Yuga will also come to an end.

This temple was built in the 6th century by the Kalchuri dynasty, but the caves of the fort were discovered in the 11th century. The Shiva Lingam inside the cave is naturally formed. This temple is situated at an altitude of 4,671 feet within the fort.

The water surrounding the Shiva Lingam in the temple is extremely cold. Taking a sacred bath in this cold water is considered spiritually significant. It is believed that bathing here cleanses all sins. To reach this temple, one must undertake trekking, which adds a new experience to the overall journey.

# The Only Temple Where One Can See All Four Dhams Together

## Patal Bhuvaneshwar Cave Temple – Uttarakhand (Pithoragarh)

Located in Gangolihaat in the Pithoragarh district of Uttarakhand, this cave is unique as it offers the opportunity to see all four Dhams together.

There are many temples and caves dedicated to Lord Shiva across the world, each famous for its own mysteries.

One such famous cave is the Patal Bhuvaneshwar Cave located in Gangolihaat, Pithoragarh, and it is said to have hidden symbols of the end of the Kali Yuga. In fact, the Patal Bhuvaneshwar Cave is located approximately 90 feet below sea level and is 160 meters long from the entrance. To visit this cave, one must enter it, not a temple, to view Lord Shiva.

According to ancient texts, it is believed that Patal Bhuvaneshwar is the only temple where devotees can see all four Dhams – Kedarnath, Badrinath, Amarnath and more. In addition to these, figures of Kedar, Badrinath, Mata Bhuvneshwari, Lord Ganesha, Lord Shiva's locks, Kund Mukti, Dwar and other deities can also be seen inside the cave. It is said that 33 categories of deities (12 Adityas, 11 Rudras, 8 Vasus and 2 Ashwini Kumars) reside in the Patal Bhuvaneshwar Temple.

> According to the legends, when Lord Shiva became angry and severed Lord Ganesha's head from his body, later, at the request of Goddess Parvati, Ganesha was given the head of an elephant. The head that Lord Shiva severed is said to be present

in the Patal Bhuvaneshwar Cave. Additionally, above the stone statue of Ganesha, there is a rock in the shape of a Brahmakamal (a sacred lotus) with 108 petals.

There are four doors in the Patal Bhuvaneshwar Temple, named Ran Dwar (War Gate), Paap Dwar (Sin Gate), Dharma Dwar (Virtue Gate), and Moksha Dwar (Liberation Gate). It is believed that after the death of Ravana, the Lord of Lanka, the Paap Dwar closed and after the Kurukshetra War, the Ran Dwar closed. Now, only two gates remain open.

The Patal Bhuvaneshwar Cave is filled with unique mysteries. It has four pillars that are associated with the four Yugas – Satya Yuga, Treta Yuga, Dwapar Yuga and Kali Yuga. Except for the pillar of Kali Yuga, no changes have occurred in the other pillars. The pillar of Kali Yuga is taller than the other three and the Shiva Lingam present here is steadily growing in size. It is believed that when the Shiva Lingam touches the ceiling of the cave, the world will come to an end.

# Cave Temples in India

## Rock-Cut Architecture

Rock-cut architecture is a type of rock art in which a solid natural rock is carved to create a structure. It is also known as cave architecture and is believed to have originated in ancient times in India. These caves were used by Buddhist and Jain monks as places of worship and residence. Initially, cave excavations were undertaken in western India.

Indian rock-cut architecture is more diverse and abundant than any other type of rock building seen worldwide (India has more than 1,500 rock-cut structures). The Mauryan Empire mastered cave architecture and are credited as the forefathers of rock-cut cave architecture. Some examples of this type of cave structure are the chaityas (prayer halls) and viharas (monasteries) of Buddhists. The Great Cave at Karla is another such example, where rocks were carved to create grand chaityas and viharas.

## History and Origin of Cave Architecture

- Since ancient times, caves in India have been regarded with reverence. The earliest caves were natural formations, used as places of worship and shelters by the original inhabitants of those regions for various purposes.
- The rock-cut designs carved into overhanging cliffs are among the earliest examples of human architectural craftsmanship on such structures. With the arrival of Buddhist missionaries, these natural caves began to be utilized as **varsa** (residences during

the monsoon season) and temples. This adaptation supported a monastic way of life in harmony with the aesthetic nature of Buddhism.

- Caves carved from massive rocks gradually evolved due to their durability compared to other construction materials like wood. Over time, these structures became more advanced and enriched architecturally.

- The earliest rock-cutting activity in the caves was observed in the western Deccan region. The initial cave temples in this area were primarily Buddhist temples and monasteries dating between 100 BCE and 170 CE. Several Jain cave basadis (pilgrimage shrines and temples) also represent early examples of rock-cut architecture.

- The Barabar Caves, located in the Jehanabad district of Bihar, India, are the oldest surviving caves in the country that showcase rock-cut architecture.

- These caves feature rock-carved Hindu and Buddhist sculptures, many of which date back to the reign of the Mauryan Empire (322–185 BCE) in the 3rd century BCE.

- Some other early cave temples reflecting cave architecture are located in Maharashtra, India. These include the Bhaja Caves (2nd century BCE), the Bedsa Caves (or Bedse, 1st century BCE), the Karla Caves (or Karle, dating between the 2nd century BCE and 5th century CE), the Kanheri Caves (developed between the 1st century BCE and 10th century CE), and some of the Ajanta Caves, which were created between the 2nd century BCE and approximately 480 or 650 CE.

## Types of Caves

1. **Buddhist Caves**
2. **Hindu Caves**
3. **Jain Caves**

## 1. Buddhist Caves

- Some of the finest examples of cave architecture can be found in ancient Buddhist caves. A significant portion of the approximately 1200 surviving cave temples is Buddhist.

- The topography of the Western Ghats, characterized by deep ravines, steep rocky expanses, and horizontal basalt hilltops, naturally attracted Buddhist monks to the region. They utilized the caves as shelters and pilgrimage sites.

- From 200 BCE to 650 CE, Buddhist monks occupied the oldest Kanheri Caves, located within the forests of the Sanjay Gandhi National Park in Maharashtra, India. These caves were carved out of a massive basaltic rock during the 1st and 2nd centuries BCE. Similarly, the oldest Ajanta Caves also date back to the 2nd century BCE.

- Among the oldest caves are cave temples associated with Buddhism, including the Karla Caves, Kanheri Caves, Bhaja Caves, Bedsa Caves, and Ajanta Caves.

- The ideology of Buddhism encouraged engagement with trade and commerce, and the early association of Buddhists with traders likely influenced them to establish their monastic establishments near major trade routes. Thus, all Buddhist caves are situated close to significant trade routes and served as halting points for many traveling merchants. Under the patronage of wealthy traders, the interiors of some caves gradually became more advanced and elaborate. This included dividing spaces for specific purposes, such as viharas (monasteries) and chaityas (prayer halls), and adorning the spaces with fine carvings, reliefs, and paintings.

- Some caves also featured elaborate facades, ornamental gateways (toranas), rounded or circular sections, and columns. The Buddhist chaityas and viharas stand as examples of early cave structures. While viharas served as residential quarters for monks, congregational worship was conducted in cave temples known as chaityas. In the sanctum sanctorum, a circular chamber with columns was carved out of the rock, allowing circumambulation around the stupa.

- The second phase of Buddhist architecture began in the 5th century CE. The most prominent aspect of the architectural designs that emerged during this period was the introduction of the image of Lord Buddha. Enormous statues of Lord Buddha in various postures, along with Jataka tales and depictions of deities associated with Buddhism, were incorporated into stupas as carvings and paintings. Statues related to Buddhism were also installed in the viharas.

| Chaitya Caves | Vihara Caves |
| --- | --- |
| Places of worship used by Buddhist monks. A relic is enshrined here, which is called a "stupa." | Residential space for Buddhist monks, also referred to as monasteries. |
| In the *Hinayana* period (Early Buddhist period), symbolic worship was practiced. Therefore, there were no images of Buddha or associated deities, but stupas were worshipped. | Found in both *Hinayana* and *Mahayana* traditions. |
| In the *Mahayana* period (Later Buddhist period), images and carvings of Buddha, associated deities, and Jataka tales were included on stupas. | In the *Hinayana* viharas, stupas were placed. In *Mahayana viharas*, images of Buddha and related deities were installed. |
| Various postures of Buddha were also depicted on stupas. | In *Mahayana viharas*, images related to Buddha's life were carved and worshipped. |

## 2. Hindu Caves

- Hindu caves located at various sites across India are, in a way, an extension of Buddhist cave architecture, with certain modifications in architecture and design to align with Hindu traditions.

- The excavation phase of these caves dates from the 4th century CE to the 8th century CE.

- The structures depict themes from the great Hindu epics like the Ramayana and the Mahabharata.

## 3. Jain Caves

♦ Although tracing the early phase of Jain cave architecture is challenging, it is generally believed to span from the 6th century CE to the 12th century CE.

♦ These caves feature highly ornate sculptures that depict stories of the Tirthankaras from the Jain pantheon.

♦ Some Jain caves also have intricately painted ceilings, such as those found in Ellora, Maharashtra, and Sittanavasal, Tamil Nadu.

## Caves Cut into Rocks

### Elephanta Caves, Mumbai

Locally known as Gharapuri Caves, the Elephanta Caves are a remarkable and intricate example of rock-cut cave temples in India. They are located on Elephanta Island, about 10 km from Mumbai city. The island consists of two groups of caves—five Hindu caves in the first group and two Buddhist caves in the second. The first, larger group contains stone sculptures carved from rock. This group represents the Shaivite Hindu sect and is dedicated to Lord Shiva. These sculptures date back to between the 5th and 8th centuries CE.

A one-hour ferry ride from Mumbai takes you to this UNESCO World Heritage Site. The entrance to the caves is through a large hall supported by massive pillars. The hall houses the Mahesamurti, a 6.3-meter-tall (18 feet) sculpture depicting Lord Shiva in his three-headed form as the Creator, Preserver, and Destroyer. In addition to this central sculpture of Lord Shiva, there are many other sculptures of Lord Shiva located on the doorways and pillars.

The Maharashtra Tourism Development Corporation (MTDC) organizes a dance festival on Elephanta Island every year in the month of February.

### Elephanta Caves

♦ The Elephanta Caves are located on Elephanta Island (also known as Gharapuri Island) of the coast of Mumbai in Western India. This small island is home to numerous ancient archaeological remains, which are the only witnesses to its complex cultural past. These archaeological remains indicate that this region was occupied as early as the 2nd century BCE.

- The Elephanta Cave Temple (on a small island off the coast of Mumbai) dates back to the 8th century CE and is similar to Ellora.

- The Elephanta caves were originally intended to be a Buddhist site but were later overtaken by Shaiva faith.

- The caves on the island are divided into two groups:
    - A collection of five Hindu caves made from rock-cut stone sculptures, mainly associated with the Shaiva sect of Hinduism and dedicated to Lord Shiva.
    - A pair of Buddhist caves spread across the island's edges, including a hilltop mound resembling a Buddhist stupa.

- Between the 14th and 17th centuries, when Portuguese ships began sailing in the Arabian Sea and started using these caves as a base, the caves suffered extensive damage.

- They caused significant damage to the statues, which was further worsened by flooding and the dripping of rainwater.

## Features of Elephanta Caves

- The caves are carved from solid basalt rock.

- The ancient sculptures show traces of paint splashes.

- The primary cave (Cave 1) is a temple complex carved from a single rock, which includes a main chamber dedicated to Lord Shiva, two side chambers, an auxiliary temple, and numerous carvings depicting various aspects of his life, such as his marriage to Parvati and the descent of the river Ganga in his hair.

- The caves are known for their distinctive sculpture style (showing slender bodies with sharp lighting and deep effects), especially the iconic three-headed figure of Shiva, resembling the Trinity of Brahma, Vishnu, and Mahesh.

- Notable sculptures include the shaking of Mount Kailash by Ravana, Shiva's Tandava dance, Ardhanarishvara, and others.

- The caves were designated as a UNESCO World Heritage Site in 1987.
- The dating of the famous Elephanta caves is still a topic of debate, with estimates ranging from the 6th to the 8th century.
- The Rashtrakuta rulers are believed to have excavated the cave temple sometime during the 8th century, which is dedicated to Lord Shiva.
- The most important cave is the Mahesha-Murti Cave.
- The main section of this cave is 27 meters square, supported by six columns in each row (except for the three open sides and the rear corridor).
- The cave contains remarkable carvings, including depictions of Ardhanarishvara, Nataraja Shiva, Ravana shaking Kailash, the beautiful Shiva (Kalyaan), the Andhakari statue (the killing of the demon Andhaka), and others.
- There are also massive figures of 'Dwarapalas' or gatekeepers, which are quite impressive.
- The main cave is famous for its carvings in honour of Shiva, worshipped in various forms and actions.
- The Sitabai Temple, located near the large cave, features a spacious prayer hall with walls covered in beautiful and intricate sculptures, which is comparatively well-preserved than other deteriorated caves.
- The overall layout of the caves extensively uses Hindu spiritual concepts and iconography.
- The main Elephanta Cave is one of the most significant collections dedicated to Shaivism, with fifteen large reliefs around the Lingam Chapel.
- Key innovations in rock-cut architecture include the layout of the caves with pillar components, the placement of the caves, division into separate sections, and the provision of a sanctuary or sanctum in the form of a 'Sabhapadma' plan.

### Badami Caves, Karnataka

The beautiful complex of Badami Caves is located in Badami, Karnataka. The temples feature the Badami Chalukya architecture, which began in the 6th century. The caves were constructed during the rule of the Chalukya Empire in the 6th century. The complex has a total of five caves. Cave I is dedicated to Lord Shiva, Cave II and III are dedicated to Lord Vishnu, and Cave IV is dedicated to Jain saints. The fifth cave was once a Buddhist temple. To enter the cave, one has to crawl due to its small dimensions. The popular Badami cave temples are a blend of North Indian Nagara and South Dravidian architectural styles. Entry Fee:

### Ajanta Caves, Aurangabad

Located in the Aurangabad district of Maharashtra, the Ajanta Caves are 30 rock-cut caves that have been declared a UNESCO World Heritage Site. These rock-cut cave temples were built 2000 years ago and still preserve the country's cultural heritage. The caves take religious influence from Buddhism and Jataka tales, which can be seen through the paintings.

All the temples in the caves are dedicated to Lord Buddha and his monasteries. This is why the caves hold significant religious importance for Buddhists. People from all over the world come to the caves to pay homage to Lord Buddha. The Ajanta Caves are considered one of the finest examples of Buddhist architecture.

[*See* also **Chapter 88**]

### Mawsmai Caves, Meghalaya

Located 6 km from Cherrapunji, the Mawsmai Caves are among the most popular caves in India, situated in the northeastern state of Meghalaya, the abode of clouds. The caves are famous for being the only caves that have ample lighting, enabling tourists to explore their natural formations. The Mawsmai Caves are natural limestone caves, making Cherrapunji a highly popular destination that tourists must visit. The length of the cave is only 150 meters, which is not very long compared to other caves. The main attraction of this cave is the flora and fauna found within it.

The cave contains several stalactites and stalagmites in various shapes and forms. These are the result of years of natural erosion and dripping water. Mawsmai Cave is an easily accessible cave and is one of the few caves in the country that can be explored without a guide.

## Bhimbetka Caves, Madhya Pradesh

A UNESCO World Heritage Site, the Bhimbetka Caves and shelters are located in the Raisen district of Madhya Pradesh. The caves take us back to the dawn of humanity through their rock paintings. This site is known for displaying the early traces of humanity on the Indian subcontinent.

That is why this area holds a significant place in the history of humankind. The caves and shelters are structures from the Stone Age, dating back nearly 30,000 years. The entire Raisen region is surrounded by dense green forests, which enhance the beauty of the place.

## Udayagiri and Khandagiri Caves, Odisha

For all history lovers, Udayagiri and Khandagiri Caves are a must-visit. These caves are famous for providing insights into India's rich past. These multi-story rock-cut caves depict the role of Jainism in the history of Odisha. The caves were specifically built for Jain monks under the orders of the great Jain king Kharavela. Although the caves were designed with engraved figures of women, elephants, flowers, and athletes, much of the artwork is no longer present in the caves. However, what remains is enough to speak about the time period. Since there are no signposts in the caves, it is best to carry a tour guide with you. Cave 4, or the Queen's Cave, has damaged the structures of that time. The main attraction of the caves is Cave 10, known as the Ganesh Cave. This cave houses a beautiful statue of Lord Ganesh.

## Ellora Caves, Aurangabad

Located in Aurangabad, the Ellora Caves are one of the largest rock-cut monastic-temple complexes of the world. Originally known as 'Verul Leni,' the Ellora Caves are a UNESCO World Heritage Site. The complex consists of 34 caves, including Hindu, Jain, and Buddhist cave temples. These cave temples were built during the 4th and 5th centuries AD. There are 12 Buddhist caves in the south, 17 Hindu caves in the center, and 5 Jain caves in the north. The main attraction of the Ellora

Caves is the Kailasa Temple, which is believed to be a replica of Lord Shiva's celestial residence on Mount Kailash.

The caves are considered one of the most remarkable examples of Indian rock-cut architecture. The Ellora Caves are famous for showcasing the craftsmanship of Indian sculptors to the world through their architecture.

### Karla Caves, Lonavala, Maharashtra

Located on the Pune-Mumbai Highway in Maharashtra, the Karla Caves are popular rock-cut cave temples. The rock-cut cave temples in India are considered some of the oldest examples of early Buddhist temple art. The entrance to the caves is grand, with a horseshoe-shaped arch. The main cave of Karla, a Chaitya, has 37 pillars and stands atop a water pot. The caves were used by Buddhist monks for spiritual retreats during that time.

The caves were constructed around 100 CE by Buddhist nuns. The Karla Caves feature beautiful carved Chaityas and Vihars. While the Chaitya was used as a prayer hall, the Vihar was where the monks resided during their entire meditation period. The length of the Chaitya hall is 45 meters and its height is 14 meters, making it one of the largest rock-cut Chaityas in India.

The walls of the Chaitya and Vihar have sculptures of animals like lions and elephants. These sculptures are adorned with metal jewellry and ivory tusks.

### Pataleshwar Cave Temple, Maharashtra

Dating back to the 8th century, the Pataleshwar Cave Temple is one of the most popular rock-cut cave temples in India. Located in the center of Pune, the Pataleshwar Cave Temple is dedicated to Lord Pataleshwar (the god of the underworld) and Lord Shiva. The temple cave is characterized by the unique sound of bells.

The architecture of the temple cave resembles that of the Elephanta Caves. The main attraction of the temple is the shrine of Lord Shiva. The pillars of the temple are extraordinary and unique. The Pataleshwar Cave Temple has a museum that is listed in the Guinness Book of Records. The museum houses a grain of rice that is believed to have around 5,000 characters engraved on it.

Another attraction of the temple is the Shiva Linga worship, which is conducted with intense devotion. Many devotees come to the temple to participate in this worship and be part of the grand celebrations.

## Borra Caves, Andhra Pradesh

Located in the Anantagiri Hills, the Borra Caves are a major attraction in Visakhapatnam, Andhra Pradesh. The Borra Caves are natural caves, believed to have been formed by the Gosthani River that flows through limestone areas. The caves feature stalactite and stalagmite formations. The Borra Caves are the largest caves in the country, located at an altitude of about 705 meters. They stretch up to a depth of 80 meters and are considered the deepest caves in India. The combination of sunlight and darkness inside the Borra Caves presents a breathtaking view, which is truly unimaginable.

When visiting Visakhapatnam, you must not miss seeing these captivating caves. Situated 1,400 meters above sea level, the Borra Caves are famous for their massive archaeological and historical significance. This site also holds historical and religious importance. In 1807, William King George of the Indian Geological Survey discovered some prehistoric tools believed to be nearly one million years old.

The caves also hold religious significance, as there is a Shiva Linga and a statue of the sacred cow Kamadhenu inside the cave, which is considered highly holy by the locals.

## Dungeshwari Cave Temple, Bihar

Popularly known as Mahakal Caves, the Dungeshwari Caves are located about 15 km from Bodh Gaya. These caves hold immense religious significance, as it is believed to be the place where Lord Buddha meditated before reaching Gaya. Today, the caves are among the most popular caves in India. Followers of Buddhism and those seeking peace of mind visit the caves for meditation.

It is believed that Lord Buddha spent several years in the Dungeshwari Caves before proceeding to Bodh Gaya. The caves now house several temples and sanctuaries dedicated to Lord Buddha, which are visited by pilgrims every day. The atmosphere of the caves is unique, and it is the main attraction of the caves.

## Belum Caves, Andhra Pradesh

The second-largest caves in India, the Belum Caves are naturally formed caves discovered by British surveyor Robert Bruce Foote in 1884. The famous Belum Caves are located in the Kurnool district of Andhra Pradesh. In 1988, a team of German archaeologists rediscovered the caves and classified them as a protected site. In 2002, these caves were opened to tourists.

With continuous flowing water over the limestone deposits in the caves, stalactites and stalagmites have formed. The caves are 3 km long, and their depth is 150 feet below the ground level. The remains in the caves date back to the Buddhist era, which certifies that Buddhist monks once resided in these caves. Some other remains suggest that the caves were inhabited as early as 4500 BCE. The Belum Caves feature an entrance hall and a sixteen-path labyrinth.

## Masroor Cave Temple, Himachal Pradesh

Located in Himachal Pradesh, the Masroor Cave Temple is also known as the Himalayan Pyramid. This rock-cut temple complex consists of 15 monolithic rock-cut monuments. Each of them is carved in the traditional Indo-Aryan style, which is very characteristic of northern India. Near this temple complex, there is a pond known as Masroor Sarovar, where the temple's reflection can be seen.

## Ramalingeshwar Cave Temple, Bengaluru

Located in the Hulima city of Bengaluru, the Ramalingeshwar Cave Temple provides a sense of peace. This cave has been in existence for 2,000 years, but the temple inside is 400 to 500 years old. The temple is dedicated to Lord Shiva, and records mention that statues of deities were placed in the temple in 1850.

## Amarnath Cave

One of India's most ancient and religious sites, the Amarnath Cave is located 135 kilometers from Srinagar, the capital of Jammu and Kashmir, at an altitude of 13,000 feet. The Amarnath Cave is the most religiously significant pilgrimage site in India. The cave is 19 meters high, 19 meters deep, and 16 meters wide, and it is famous for the naturally ice-formed Shiva Linga. Due to the natural and miraculous formation of the Shiva Linga, it is also called the Barfaani Baba or

Himani Shiva Linga. Every year, millions of tourists visit this sacred cave as part of the Amarnath Yatra. The Amarnath Cave is considered an important place for pilgrims.

## Bhimbetka Caves, Madhya Pradesh

The Bhimbetka Caves, located in Bhiyanpura, Raisen district of Madhya Pradesh, provide a unique glimpse into the prehistoric era of India. The Bhimbetka Caves are like a natural gallery that showcases paintings from the prehistoric period to the medieval era. Bhimbetka is one of the UNESCO World Heritage Sites and was declared a World Heritage Site in 2003.

These caves are located on one of the seven hills, and there are more than 750 rock shelters spread across an area of about 10 kilometers. Visiting this site and viewing the caves is no less than an adventurous task, as it preserves art-rich rock shelters, the Bhimbetka Fort, and remains of mini stupas, which point towards Buddhist influences. Several inscriptions have also been found here, dating back to an uncertain period, including the Shunga, Kushana, and Gupta eras. Bhimbetka is an ideal place for history enthusiasts and is indeed one of the best places to visit in Madhya Pradesh.

## Bag Caves, Madhya Pradesh

The Bag Caves are located in the Vindhyachal mountain range on the banks of the Baghani River in Madhya Pradesh. These caves are a group of nine rock-cut structures, believed to have been created by the Buddhist monk Dattaka during the 4th to 6th century CE. The caves still display beautiful ancient paintings, which is why the Bag Caves are also known as "Rang Mahal" (Color Palace). These rock-cut caves are an unparalleled example of ancient Indian art, attracting numerous tourists and art lovers.

## Udaygiri and Khandagiri Caves, Bhubaneswar

The ancient Udaygiri caves are located near Bhubaneswar in the state of Odisha. The Udaygiri caves are famous for their 33 rock-cut chambers that showcase Hindu and Jain sculptures and wall paintings. The history of these caves dates back to the Gupta period, around 350-550 CE, a time that laid the foundation of Hindu religious thoughts. The most famous structure in the Udaygiri cave is a 5-foot-high statue of Vishnu's *Varaha avatar*, with devotees standing by its sides. These caves are situated about 6 kilometers from Bhubaneswar. It is believed that these caves are some of the earliest caves built by the Jain community. There are 18 caves in Udaygiri and 15 caves in Khandagiri, with the Queen's Cave being considered the most special.

### Undadalli Caves, Andhra Pradesh

Located 8 kilometers from Vijayawada city in Andhra Pradesh, the Undadalli Caves are situated on the banks of the Krishna River. These caves were built by the Vishnukundin kings in the 7th century CE. It is believed that the ancient caves were carved out of solid sandstone and are dedicated to Anantapadmanabha Swamy and Narasimha Swamy. The Undadalli Caves are among the finest cave structures found in India. These caves are a seamless example of Indian rock-cut architecture, attracting not only tourists but also a large number of researchers and art enthusiasts.

### Varaha Caves, Tamil Nadu

The Varaha Caves, located in Mahabalipuram, Tamil Nadu, are a cave temple dedicated to the avatar of Lord Vishnu, "Varaha." The famous Varaha Cave temple in Mahabalipuram includes a mandapa (hall) along with a solid rock-cut temple. Like other caves in this region, this cave was built in the 7th century and is carved into the rocky walls of a granite hill. It is known for its grand architecture and is listed as a UNESCO World Heritage Site. The walls of the mandapa depict Lord Vishnu in the form of Varaha, with a statue of Bhudevi (Earth Goddess) alongside him. These caves serve as an important pilgrimage site, attracting tourists and devotees from various corners of the country.

### Jogimara Caves, Chhattisgarh

Located in the dense forests of Chhattisgarh, the Jogimara Caves are among the ancient caves of India. These caves can be reached through a natural tunnel called Hatipol, which is so wide that even elephants can pass through it, as implied by the name. The Jogimara Caves are believed to date back to the Treta Yuga, and it is said that Lord Ram, Sita, and Lakshman spent some time here during their exile. The caves are filled with ancient paintings and inscriptions that provide evidence of Lord Ram, Sita, and Lakshman's stay in the area.

Kashi Vishwanath Temple - Uttar Pradesh (Varanasi)

Ratneshwar Mahadev Temple - Uttar Pradesh (Varanasi)

## Tabo Caves, Himachal Pradesh

The Tabo Caves are located right above the ancient Tabo Monastery, which was established more than 1,000 years ago. These caves, located near Tabo village, were carved out of the hills and are believed to have served as a meditation place for Buddhist monks. There are some larger caves along with smaller ones, and these caves are still used by Buddhist monks for meditation during the winter months. That's why many of the caves have flags attached to them, indicating that someone is meditating inside.

## Trichy Caves, Madurai

Located inside the Tiruchirapalli Rock Fort complex, the Trichy Caves are a group of two cave temples, making them one of the most remarkable cave temples in India. These cave temples are known as the Lower Cave Temple and the Upper Cave Temple. It is believed that the Trichy Caves were constructed by the Pallava, Chola, and Nayak rulers of Madurai. The temples in these unfinished caves include a temple to Lord Shiva in the east and a temple to Lord Vishnu in the west, while the lower caves are marked by a unique form of columns.

## Sithanavasal Caves, Tamil Nadu

Located in Sithanavasal village in Pudukkottai district, Tamil Nadu, the Sithanavasal Caves are among the oldest caves in India, also known as Arivar Koli. According to researchers, the Sithanavasal Caves date back to around the 7th century. These caves are famous for their various paintings, including images of people collecting lotus flowers from a pond, along with pictures of lilies, fish, buffaloes, and elephants.

## Koteshwar Cave

One of the oldest caves in India, the Koteshwar Cave is located about 3 kilometers from Rudraprayag in Uttarakhand. The Koteshwar Caves serve as an important pilgrimage site for Hindus. According to mythological legends, it is believed that when Bhasmasura chased Lord Shiva to burn him, Lord Shiva meditated in this cave. The cave is a popular Hindu pilgrimage site where devotees come year-round, with August and September seeing an especially large crowd of worshippers.

### Patal Bhubaneswar Caves, Uttarakhand

One of the most popular religious caves in India, the Patal Bhubaneswar Caves are located in Bhubaneswar village near Gangolihat in Uttarakhand. It is believed that these caves were discovered by King Ritupurna of the Solar Dynasty during the Treta Yuga. It is also believed that there were four doors to enter the cave, named 'Randwar' (War Gate), 'Papdwar' (Sin Gate), 'Dharmdwar' (Religion Gate), and 'Mokshdwar' (Moksha Gate). According to Hindu mythology, Papdwar was closed shortly after the death of Ravana, and Randwar was closed after the Mahabharata war. Therefore, only two entrance gates are currently open. These caves are considered to be the home of all Hindu deities. Additionally, various limestone rock formations can be seen here.

### Krem Liat Prah

Krem Liat Prah, located in the Shongrim Ridge of the East Jaintia Hills district in the state of Meghalaya, North India, is the longest natural cave in India and one of the 150 known caves in the region. The word "Krem" in the Meghalaya language means "cave." It is one of the longest caves in the world, with an estimated length of 34 kilometers.

### Barabar Caves, Bihar

The Barabar Caves are among the oldest caves in India, located between the Nagarjuni hills in Bihar. These are rock-cut caves, and this collection consists of four caves: Lomash Rishi Cave, Sudama Cave, Karan Chaupar, and Vishwajyopari. Most of these caves belong to the Maurya Empire (322-185 BCE), and some of the caves also contain inscriptions from the Ashokan period. All of these caves are attractive in their own way, with the Lomash Rishi Caves resembling the huts where Buddhist monks used to live, while the Sudama Cave has an arch-like structure. There are some fascinating stories related to these caves that excite everyone to visit them.

### Kutumsar Caves, Chhattisgarh

Located in the Kanger Valley National Park in Bastar, Chhattisgarh, the Kutumsar Caves are prehistoric caves famous for their stalactite and stalagmite formations. At the end of the Kutumsar Cave, there is a Shivling (a sacred symbol of Lord Shiva), which attracts both tourists and many religious followers to the site. The Kutumsar Cave is 1327 meters long and has five naturally formed chambers and a well inside, both of which contribute significantly to the cave's attraction.

## Nellitheertha Cave, Karnataka

Located in the South Kanara district of Karnataka, the Nellitheertha Cave is one of the most prominent caves in India. The Nellitheertha Cave is a 200-meter-long temple cave that is naturally formed. Inside the cave, there is a pond and a Shivling. It is believed that the Shivling originated from water droplets dripping inside the cave. The word "Nellitheertha" is derived from the Kannada language, where "Nelli" means "amla" (gooseberry) and "theertha" means "holy water." Therefore, the cave is named Nellitheertha Cave. This cave is one of India's famous religious sites, attracting a large number of pilgrims.

## Saptaparni Cave

- Saptaparni Cave, also known as Saptaparni Cave (in Saraiki) or Sattapani Guha (in Pali), is actually a cave with seven leaves, located about 2 kilometers (1.2 miles) southwest of Rajgir in Bihar.

- It is embedded in a hill. The Saptaparni Cave is significant in Buddhist tradition because many believe that this is the place where Buddha spent some time before his death, and where the first Buddhist council was held after Buddha's death (Parinirvana).

- Here, a council of several hundred monks decided to appoint Ananda (Buddha's cousin) and Upali to compose Buddha's teachings for future generations, as they were believed to have excellent memory and had been with Buddha while he preached in Northern India.

- Buddha himself never wrote down his teachings. After the meeting at the Saptaparni Caves, Ananda created an oral tradition of Buddha's teachings from his memory, with the preface "I heard this on one occasion."

- Upali is credited with teaching the Nikaya discipline or "rules for monks.'

## Barabar Caves

- The Barabar Hill Caves are the oldest surviving rock-cut caves in India, dating back to the Maurya period (322-185 BCE). Some of them bear Ashokan inscriptions and are located in the Makhdumpur area of Jehanabad district in Bihar, about 24 kilometers (15 miles) north of Gaya.

- These caves are situated in the twin hills of Barabar (four caves) and Nagarjuni (three caves); the caves on Nagarjuni Hill, located 1.6 kilometers (0.99 miles) away, are sometimes recognized as the Nagarjuni Caves.

- The chambers carved out of the rocks have inscriptions dedicated to "King Piyadasi" for the Barabar group and "Devanampiya Dasharatha" for the Nagarjuni group, which are believed to date from the third century BCE during the Maurya period, and correspond to Ashoka (reign: 273-232 BCE) and his grandson, Dasharatha Maurya, respectively.

- The caves of Barabar Hill are the oldest rock-cut caves in the world. These caves were carved out of a single solid piece of granite.

- The sculptures around the entrance of the Lomash Rishi Cave represent the oldest existence of the "Chaitya Arches" or "Chandrashala" in the shape of a bird, which was an important feature in Indian rock-cut architecture and sculptural decoration for centuries. This form clearly represents the reconstruction of buildings made of stone from wood and other plant materials.

## Features of Barabar Caves

- Emperor Ashoka had the Barabar Caves constructed for the benefit of the Ajivika ascetics, and thus, it is known as the birthplace of the Ajivika sect.

- The Barabar Hill caves are Buddhist caves. However, some Hindu and Jain statues can also be found. The Nagarjuni Hills (which include three caves) are located 2 kilometers away from the Barabar Hill Caves (which include four caves).

- These caves are referred to as 'Satghar' because they are considered to belong to the same time period.
- The Baba Siddhnath Temple, also known as the Shiva Temple and formerly known as the Siddheshwar Nath Temple, is located on one of the highest peaks of the Barabar Hills.
- It is believed that this temple was constructed during the Gupta dynasty.
- All the caves in Barabar exhibit fascinating echo effects.

**Caves of Barabar Hill**

- There are four caves on Barabar Hill: Karan Choupad, Lomash Rishi, Sudama, and Vishwakarma.
- Sudama and Lomash Rishi are among the earliest examples of rock-cut architecture in India, detailing the architecture of the Maurya period. Similar examples can be found in larger Buddhist chaityas in Maharashtra, such as the Ajanta and Karla Caves. The Barabar Caves significantly influenced the tradition of rock-cut architecture in the Indian subcontinent.

**Lomash Rishi Caves**

- The human-made Barabar Caves, also called the Lomash Rishi's kuti, are located on the southern edge of Barabar Hills.
- Carved from rocks, the Lomash Rishi Cave was created as an asylum.
- It contains the oldest surviving example of the Dwija-shaped Chandrashala or Chaitya arch, which has long been a popular feature in Indian sculpture and rock-cut buildings.
- The arched facade of the Lomash Rishi Cave is an ideal representation of the wooden and thatched huts of monks.
- The Lomash Rishi Cave is divided into two rooms. After passing through a short tunnel, a large rectangular hall comes into view, serving as an assembly hall.
- A second, smaller hall with an oval-shaped interior and a dome-shaped roof lies ahead.

- The internal surfaces of the chambers have a brilliant glass-like shine and are beautifully crafted. This is a common feature in the Barabar Caves.
- This cave served as a model for large Buddhist chaitya halls like those in the Ajanta or Karla Caves in Maharashtra, and had a significant impact on the South Asian rock-cut building heritage.
- The excavation of Lomash Rishi Cave was granted to the Ajivika monks during the reign of Mauryan ruler Ashoka.
- Ajivika was an ancient Indian religious and philosophical sect that competed with Jainism and eventually became extinct. They rejected both the Vedic proofs and Buddhist beliefs, and meditated in these caves.
- Inscriptions of elephants and other symbols can be seen on the cave walls and the entrance of the Chaitya arch. There is no Ashokan inscription in the Lomash Rishi Cave.
- After the Ajivikas, Buddhists began using the Lomash Rishi Cave as well, as Bodhimula and Klesa-Kantara inscriptions are found on the doorway of the cave.
- According to an inscription on the torana, a Hindu ruler from the Maukari dynasty, Anantavarman, dedicated a statue of Lord Krishna in the cave.

**Sudama Caves**
- The Sudama Caves are located on the left side of the Barabar Hills, near the Lomash Rishi Caves.
- According to an inscription near the entrance of the Sudama Cave, it was possibly the first cave to be carved in the Barabar Cave complex.
- Emperor Ashoka donated the Sudama Cave, as indicated by an inscription in Brahmi at the entrance, showing his official name (Priyadarshin, "One who is liked by everyone").
- The entrance to the Sudama Cave leads to a rectangular path.
- The roof of the Sudama Cave is arched. Inside, there is a domed circular room with a rectangular hall within.

- The internal walls of the Sudama Caves are an engineering marvel. The granite surfaces are exceptionally flat and polished, giving a mirror-like reflection.
- Between the two rooms, there is a central doorway with an unusual upper semicircular section, which is curved and slanted towards the center, resembling the roofs of native bamboo and thatched houses.

## Vishwakarma Cave

- Like the other Barabar Caves, the Vishwakarma Cave also consists of two rectangular rooms. One of the rooms, like a verandah, is fully open from the outside.
- The cave is also referred to as the Vishwamitra Caves.
- "Ashoka Stairs" carved into the rock provide access to this cave.
- In the 12th year of Ashoka's reign, he provided the Vishwakarma Cave to the Ajivikas.
- This is the only cave in the series that does not have any inscriptions from the period after Ashoka's reign.
- Emperor Ashoka dedicated the Vishwakarma Cave in 260 BCE, and seven years later, he dedicated the Karan Choupar Cave, which is located a little distance away from the Vishwakarma Cave.

## Karan Choupar Cave

- Karan Choupar is located on the northern edge of Barabar Hills.
- There is an inscription from the 19th year of Ashoka's reign on this cave.
- An inscription found at the entrance of the cave describes the Buddhist practice of retreating (Vasavasa) during the monsoon season.
- The inverted swastika at the end of the inscription indicates that this cave, one of the four equal caves, was reserved for Buddhist monks.

- Near the entrance, a mound covered with later Buddhist sculptures indicates that the cave was once a Buddhist site.
- At one end of the cave, there is a carved rock space. It consists of a single rectangular room with shining surfaces.
- An inscription from the Gupta dynasty in the entrance chamber mentions "Daridra Kantara" ("Cave of the poor").

**Nagarjun Caves**

- The caves near Nagarjun Hill were created a few decades after the Barabar Caves and were sanctified by Ashoka's grandson and successor, Dasharatha Maurya. These caves are located 1.6 kilometers east of the Barabar caves.
- Three caves have been carved into Nagarjun Hills: Vedathi-ka-Kumbh (Vedathmika Kumbha), Wapiya-ka-Kumbh (Mirza Mandi), and Gopi-ka-Kubha.
- The largest cave is the Gopi Cave or Milkmaid Cave.
- Gopi (Gopi-ka-Kubha, Doodhwali) is a cave that can be reached by climbing large steps. It has the largest chamber in the group. The cave has several important inscriptions, some of which indicate that Ashoka's son Dasharatha (who reigned from 232 - 224 BCE) dedicated these caves to the Ajivikas. These structures may be about 50 years younger than the Barabar caves. The cave is 12.3 meters long and 5.8 meters wide, with semi-circular ends. The roof is dome-shaped, reaching up to 3.2 meters high. The walls and floor of the cave are polished, showing the famous "Mauryan polish."
- To the north of Nagarjun Cave, there is another cave – Mirza Mandi (Mirza's House). Nearby, there is a dry well, which suggests its alternative name "Well Cave" or Vahiya-ka-Kubha, Wapiya-ka-Kubha. Several other remains of structures are found nearby, possibly belonging to a vihara (Buddhist temple).
- The cave has an inscription: "Vahiya Cave was dedicated to the esteemed Ajivikas by Dasharatha shortly after his consecration." Other caves have similar inscriptions, with different names for the caves.

## Pitalkhora Caves

- The Pitalkhora Caves, located in the Satmala Range of Maharashtra's Western Ghats, are an ancient Buddhist site with 14 rock-cut caves. These caves date back to the 3rd century BCE, making them one of the earliest examples of rock-cut architecture in India.

- Located about 40 kilometers from Ellora, the caves can be reached via a steep climb of concrete steps, passing by a waterfall.

- The caves have been carved out of various basalt rocks, but some caves are damaged. Out of the 14 caves, four are chaityas (one housing a stupa, one semi-circular, and a single-cell chaitya), and the rest are viharas.

- All the caves belong to the early Buddhist schools, but the well-preserved paintings date to the Mahayana period.

- The caves are grouped into two sets: one with 10 caves and the other with 4 caves. It is believed that Pitalkhora may be identified with Ptolemy's "Petrigala" and the Buddhist chronicle "Pitanglya" from Mahamayuri. The inscriptions are dated from 250 BCE to the 3rd and 4th centuries CE.

- The site features statues of elephants, two soldiers (one of which is intact), a damaged Gaj Lakshmi icon, and an ancient rainwater harvesting system. These caves have been significant in establishing the chronological sequence of cave construction in the Ajanta-Ellora region.

## Kondana Caves (Raigad, Maharashtra)

- The Kondana Caves are located 33 kilometers north of Lonavala and 16 kilometers northwest of the Karla Caves, in the small village of Kondana.

- This cave complex consists of 16 Buddhist caves. The caves were excavated in the 1st century BCE, and the construction shows remarkable wooden patterns.

- The only inscription found at the entrance of the cave is a chaitya inscription, providing information about the donors.

## Bhaja Caves

- The Bhaja Caves, located near Pune city, are a group of 22 rock-cut caves dating back to the 2nd century BCE.
- These caves are associated with the early Buddhist schools of Maharashtra. The caves contain many stupas, which are among their most important features. The most notable excavation is the chaitya (or Chaityagriha - Cave XII), which is a good example of the early development of wooden architecture in stone, with a vaulted horseshoe-shaped roof.
- In front of its vihara (Cave XVIII) is a portico with columns, which is uniquely adorned with carvings. These caves are remarkable for showing awareness of wooden architecture.
- The Bhaja Caves share architectural designs with the Karla Caves. The most impressive monument is a large temple, a chaityagriha, with an open, horseshoe-shaped arch entrance.

## Features of Bhaja Caves

- The Bhaja Caves represent the *Hinayana* sect of Buddhism.
- The architectural design of the Bhaja Caves is similar to that of the Karla Caves.
- Their elaborate form has made them famous.
- The most unique feature of the caves is that the rays of the setting sun penetrate deep inside the caves.
- The stupas, numbering 14 and arranged in a cluster, are one of the most notable features of the cave.
- It is believed that the relics of the monks who lived and died in the Bhaja Caves are contained within these stupas.
- Two of the stupas have a relic box at the top, and all of them are intricately carved.
- Out of the 14 stupas, five are inside smaller caves, while the remaining nine are outside.
- Beautiful garlands, necklaces, and jewellry adorn the statues inside the Bhaja Buddhist kuti (monastic chambers).

- There are depictions of several animals and inscriptions with the names of Buddhist monks, along with some images of the Buddha.
- A *chaityagriha* (prayer hall), unique to the cave, is surrounded by 27 columns, and the roof has wooden beams.
- The roof beams are real, which is a unique feature.
- With an open, horseshoe-arched entrance, this is the most impressive and expansive pilgrimage chaityagriha.
- The chaityagriha has wooden architectural models and a domed horseshoe-shaped ceiling. Another interesting aspect of the cave is its wooden construction.
- Inscriptions confirm that the tabla, a percussion instrument, was used in India for at least two centuries. One carving shows a woman playing the tabla while another woman is dancing.
- Simple rock-cut vihara (residential chambers) have been made, and water tanks can be found in the Bhaja Buddhist complex.
- The viharas are adorned with unique carvings and have porticos with columns in front of them.
- The viharas at Bhaja are divided into two levels. Some of the viharas have two stories. Only one vihara in Bhaja is adorned with sculptural decorations.
- One of the carvings depicts a woman playing the tabla and another dancing, indicating that the tabla (or its earlier form) has been used in India for more than 2,000 years.
- Near the last cave, there is a magnificent waterfall, and the water flows into a small lake during the monsoon season.
- The Archaeological Survey of India (ASI) has declared the inscriptions and cave temples as monuments of national importance.

## Karla Caves

- The Karla Caves, also known as Karli Caves or Karla Cell, are an ancient group of Buddhist rock-cut caves located in Karli, Maharashtra.

- They are situated just 10.9 kilometers from Lonavala. Other nearby caves include the Bhaja Caves, Patan Buddhist Caves, Bedse Caves, and Nasik Caves.
- The construction of the pilgrimage sites spans from the 2nd century BCE to the 5th century CE. It is said that the oldest cave temples were constructed around 160 BCE, strategically located along an important ancient trade route that ran from the Arabian Sea to the Deccan Plateau.
- The first sacred Karla Cave was a natural cave, but subsequently, man-made caves were created.
- The caves are traditionally associated with the Mahasanghika Buddhist sect, which gained widespread popularity and financial support in this region of India.
- Inside the caves is a Buddhist monastery dating back to the 2nd century BCE.
- South Asia's largest cave, which was constructed between 50-70 BCE and 120 BCE, was built during the reign of the Western Kshatrapa ruler Nahapana, who documented the cave's dedication in an inscription.
- The Karla Caves are among the oldest and smallest of the rock-cut Buddhist sites in Maharashtra, but they are the most famous due to the "grand chaitya" hall.
- This is considered "the largest and best-preserved chaitya hall" of its time, with an unusually large number of fine sculptures, most of which are monumental in scale.
- The construction of the caves was aided by several merchants.
- The Buddhist monastic facilities were located close to the main trade routes and situated in natural geographical formations, connecting commerce and construction through their early association with merchants, providing accommodation for traveling traders.

**Karla Caves - Features**

- The excavation of these caves took place from the 1st century CE to the 5th and 6th centuries CE.

- The largest Hinayana Buddhist chaitya (temple) in India is the Karla Cave.
- With only 15 caves, the Karla Caves are one of the most prominent Buddhist rock-cut cave sites in India.
- The main chaitya hall is one of the largest chaitya halls in India. It is important in terms of architecture, sculpture, and inscriptions.
- The Great Chaitya (Cave No. 8) in Karla is the largest rock-cut chaitya in India, measuring 45 meters (148 feet) long and 14 meters (46 feet) high.
- The grand chaitya includes massive pillars (square, stepped chairs) adorned with sculptures of men and women riding lions, elephants, and other animals, and a stupa at the center.
- The Karla Caves are distinguished by large horseshoe-shaped windows that illuminate the interior and the vaulted ceiling.
- There are two pillars, 15 meters tall, outside the chaitya, but only one remains today. The tops of the pillars are adorned with four lions.
- At the entrance to the main chaitya, there is a temple dedicated to a local goddess (temple of Devi Ekvira).
- Rows of pillars divide the chaitya into three sections: the central chamber and narrow side corridors, which are separated by two rows of intricately carved pillars, each with 15 pillars.
- Beautiful capitals adorn the pillars, depicting men and women riding elephants, and showing the Buddha in various postures, along with other depictions. By the 7th century CE, images of the Buddha were added.
- Unlike some other cave temples, the ceiling of Karla Cave No. 12 is made of wood rather than stone ribs.
- This wooden work (the canopy) is unique; the wood was cut about 2,000 years ago and has been well-preserved with no signs of rust.
- The temple, which has a canopy stupa, is located at the far end of the chaitya.

- The sculptures of Karla Cave can be seen inside the chaitya hall and on the columns of the portico.
- After the 5th century BCE, many sculptures of the Buddha and Bodhisattvas were carved in the portico.
- The sculptures of Karla represent new trends in Indian art, featuring more plasticity, with figures nearly 60% free from the wall behind them. The sculptures are refined, showing details like the folds of clothing, earrings, etc.
- Some remnants of 5th and 6th century CE paintings can be found on the pillars of the room. Several of the room's pillars have inscriptions in Brahmi script and Prakrit language, listing the names of the donors and their origins.
- The construction of the caves was assisted by many merchants and Satavahana kings.
- Long inscriptions written by royal families from the 1st to the 2nd century can also be found.

**Kanheri Caves**

- The Kanheri Caves are a collection of over 100 Buddhist caves located in the tranquil environment of Sanjay Gandhi National Park in Borivali, Mumbai. Kanheri, also known as Krishna Giri or Kanha Giri in ancient inscriptions, literally means "black mountain" (Krishna meaning "black" and Giri meaning "mountain"), named after the black basalt stone.
- These caves contain Buddhist sculptures, relief carvings, paintings, and inscriptions dating from the 1st century BCE to the 11th century CE.
- The geography of the Western Ghats, along with political patronage, favoured the construction of Buddhist caves in several hills, valleys, and rocks of the Sahyadri mountain range.
- These caves are among the earliest examples of rock-cut architecture in the Western Ghats.
- Historians suggest that the caves were excavated between 200 and 600 CE.

- Kanheri was an important monastic settlement that existed from the 1st century CE to the 11th century CE.
- During the time of the Maurya and Kushan empires, Kanheri became a center of learning.
- Due to its proximity to ancient port cities like Sopara (Nalasopara, known for its trade links with Mesopotamia and Egypt), Kalyan, Thane, and Vasai, Kanheri flourished for almost a millennium.
- Most of these caves do not have known dates, but inscriptions mentioning the names of donors and specific kings have helped identify them.
- By 1560, Buddhism gradually faded in Maharashtra, leading to the abandonment of the caves. They remained in a dilapidated state for 300 to 400 years.
- After India's independence, the Archaeological Survey of India decided to manage, revive, and preserve the heritage site.

**Kanheri Caves - Features**

- Kanheri is home to both chaitya (prayer halls) and vihara (monasteries). When they were constructed, the elements of wooden architecture were kept in mind.
- The caves are the only place in Western India where the artistic evidence of all three branches of Buddhism — Hinayana, Mahayana, and Vajrayana — are found.
- In Kanheri, Buddhist monks lived in 109 caves, where they studied, meditated, and spread the teachings of Gautama Buddha.
- During the monsoon season, the caves were also used as shelters.
- Kanheri is a collection of rock-cut monuments, a form of Western Indian traditional art.
- It also includes symbolism from the later periods of Buddhist art.
- Inside the Kanheri caves, there is a large vihara (prayer hall) and stupas (dome-shaped temples).
- The caves contain about 109 Buddha viharas, especially created for monks. The prayer halls have colonnaded corridors and excellent remains of Buddha and Bodhisattva sculptures.

- Cave Number 3 - In Kanheri, this cave contains the most well-preserved carvings. It also has a prayer hall known as the Chaitya Griha.
- The prayer hall appears majestic, with intricately carved Buddhist statues, including those with arched eye-brows and delicate, slender figures, and stupas (dome-shaped temples).
- It has a hall with 34 pillars and two large standing Buddha statues. It also shows signs of the Theravada (Hinayana) Buddhist sect.
- Cave Number 11 - This cave is quite similar to Cave Number 5 at Ellora, Aurangabad. These are the only caves in India where Buddhist monks performed collective recitation of religious texts.
- For their daily practice, they sat around long rectangular tables, carved out of the rock. The tables are still intact today.
- The monks of the caves maintained close contact with monks in China through the Silk Route, an ancient international highway that facilitated the spread of Buddha's teachings throughout Asia.
- Cave Number 41 - This cave is home to the 11-headed Avalokiteshvara, representing the compassion of all Buddhas. It is the first and only archaeological piece of this deity in India and also the oldest documented piece in the world.
- Cave Number 90 - This is the oldest cave and the only one with two Japanese inscriptions carved on its verandah. It is also the first structure in the world dedicated to the Lotus Sutra, a Buddhist teaching as given by Gautama Buddha at the end of his life.
- Kanheri caves contain a massive Buddha statue (22 feet tall) and a Chaitya Griha, which depicts a large 11-headed Avalokiteshvara (Bodhisattva), with its ceiling painted with Nada.
- It also has a developed and complex water management system, indicated by the presence of water tanks in almost every cave and large water reservoirs.

Unakoti Rock Temple - Tripura (Agartala)

Ramappa Temple - Telangana (Mulugu)

- The inscription related to the marriage of Satavahana ruler Vashisthaputra Satakarni, to the daughter of King Rudradaman I is also notable.
- Kanheri caves contain the oldest images of Buddha in South India and became world-famous after being visited by the Chinese monk Xuanzang (602 CE - 664 CE) in the 7th century CE. He is said to have taken a wooden image of Avalokiteshvara and several Sanskrit Buddhist manuscripts to China.
- Wooden architectural elements were used in the construction of Chaityas and Viharas.
- The preservation of Kanheri caves can be traced back to the Kushan and Maurya dynasties, which ruled from the 2nd century BCE to the 9th century CE. These caves were later influenced by Gupta art.
- The influence of Kanheri caves can also be seen on the magnificent Elephanta caves.
- The Buddhist group includes the Kanheri caves, Magathen caves, and Mahakali caves.
- The Magathen caves (6 km west of the Kanheri caves) are known for their excellent Makara decorations, which have now deteriorated.
- Some sculptures discovered in the Magathen caves date back to the 6th century BCE.

## Junagadh Caves

- The Junagadh Buddhist cave group is located in the Junagadh district of Gujarat, India. This cave group includes the Uparkot caves, Khapra Kodiya caves, and Baba Pyare caves.
- The so-called "Buddhist caves" are not actual caves but three separate rooms made of stone, used as residences for monks.
- The carvings in these caves were made from the time of Emperor Ashoka to the 1st-4th century CE.

## Uparkot

- The Uparkot caves, located near Adi Kadi Baw, across a 300-feet deep gorge, were constructed during the 2nd-3rd century CE.

- These caves exhibit a blend of Greco-Scythian style with the influence of Satavahana architecture.

**Khapra Kodiya Caves**

- The oldest, Khapra Kodiya Caves, based on inscriptions written on the walls and small scratched letters, date back to the 3rd-4th century BCE during the reign of Emperor Ashoka and are the simplest among all the cave groups. These caves are also known as Khangar Mahal.
- They were carved into living rock during the reign of Emperor Ashoka and are considered the oldest monastic settlement in the region.
- These caves are located near the ancient Sudarshan Lake, slightly to the north of the Uparkot fort.
- They are carved in an east-west longitudinal manner. The caves are small in area, but the design of water tanks on the western side and the 'L'-shaped residence is a unique architectural feature.

**Baba Pyare Caves**

- The Baba Pyare Caves are located just outside the Uparkot Fort complex, towards the south, near Modhimath. These are much more well-preserved compared to the Khapra Kodiya Caves.
- The caves were built during the Satavahana rule in the 1st-2nd century CE.
- According to the travelogue of Xuanzang, these caves were constructed in the 1st century CE.
- The Baba Pyare Caves contain artwork from both Buddhist and Jain religions.

**Nashik Caves (Pandav leni Caves)**

- The Pandavleni Caves, also known as Trirashmi Caves, are ancient rock-cut caves located on the Trirashmi Hill, about 3004 feet above sea level. These are a collection of ancient Hinayana Buddhist caves (BCE 250 - CE 600).

- The caves of Nashik are another name for them. Recently, the Archaeological Survey of India (ASI) discovered three new caves in the Trirashmi Buddhist cave complex.

- Captain James Delamain first documented the Trirashmi Buddhist cave complex in 1823, and it is now an ASI-protected site.

- "Leni" is a Marathi word for caves. The Pandavleni Caves consist of 24 carved cave temples known as Viharas. Chaitya is one of the 24 carved cave temples.

- In ancient times, these viharas functioned as monasteries where people could meet monks and discuss, while the viharas also served as prayer halls for Buddhist monks and disciples of Gautama Buddha.

- The carvings in these caves were made between the 1st and 3rd centuries BCE, with additional sculptures added up to the 6th century, reflecting the changes in Buddhist devotional practices.

- Except for Cave 18, which is a chaitya from the 1st century BCE, most of the caves are viharas.

- The oldest cave, Number 19, was built in the 1st century BCE with the donation of the Satavahana ruler Krishna.

- Some of the more complex styles of columns or pillars, as seen in Caves 3 and 10, are a good example of how the design evolved.

- Inscriptions that document contributions date the caves to the 1st century BCE.

- The caves were named Pundru, meaning "yellow ochre" in Pali. This name was given because the caves were home to Buddhist monks who wore "chivara" or yellow robes. Later, the name Pundru was changed to Pandu Caves (according to the Ancient Monuments Preservation Act, 1904).

- Cave evidence shows that the caves are a testimony to the period between the Satavahanas and the Western Kshatrapas, who ruled the region in the 1st century CE.

- After the decline of Buddhism, Jainism took over the site. During the medieval period, Jain monasteries were likely present as well.

## Features

- The Pandavleni Caves are a collection of ancient Buddhist caves.
- The Kshatrapas, Satavahanas, and Abhiras—three kings who once ruled Nashik—are depicted in these caves.
- The Pandavleni Caves are a group of 24 Buddhist caves belonging to the Hinayana sect of Buddhism.
- All the caves are intricate carvings and excellent examples of craftsmanship, but Caves Number 3, 10, and 18 are especially noteworthy for their exquisite sculptures.
- Water leakage is a major issue in the region, which becomes even more severe during the monsoon season. As a result, some caves have been converted into water reservoirs. One such example is Cave Number 1.
- Cave Number 2 was originally constructed as a vihara (residential quarters) in the 1st and 2nd centuries CE, and was later transformed into a temple housing the life of the Buddha.
- Cave Number 3 is one of the most striking, as it is magnificently adorned. It has six large dwarfs (door guardians). Inscriptions mention that Gautamiputra Satakarni's mother, Gautami Bala Sri, financed the construction of the third cave.
- Two of the twenty-four caves are particularly prominent:
- The main cave (Cave Number 18), which is a Chaitya (prayer hall), contains a grand stupa. These pillars are unique because they have vertical inscriptions carved on them.
- Cave Number 10, known as "Naphan Vihara," is complete in both structural and inscriptional details.
- The Trirashmi Caves are a magnificent example of detailed carvings and craftsmanship, with outstanding sculptures.
- The caves feature not only magnificent Buddha statues but also images of Vrishabha Dev, Bodhisattva symbols, and important Jain Tirthankaras like Veer Manibhadrji and Ambikadevi.
- The inscriptions in the Nashik Caves mention the kings of Western Maharashtra, the Kshatrapa dynasty, the Satavahana dynasty,

theviharas of the caves, pilgrimage sites, the mining of chaityas and kundas, and the gifting of a village to the residents of Nashik.

- The caves had excellent water management systems, with water tanks exquisitely carved into the rocks.
- Cave Number 11, the "Jain Cave," contains an inscription stating that it was a gift from the son of a writer: "A gift from Ramanak, son of the writer Shivamitra."
- Cave Number 12 contains an inscription mentioning that it was a gift from a merchant named Ramanak.

**Carvings of Jain Tirtheskaras**

- Cave Number 17, "Yavan Vihara," was constructed by a devotee of Greek origin, who presents his father as a Yavan from the northern city of Demetriapolis.
- Cave Number 19, "Krishna Vihara," contains an inscription of the Satavahana king Krishna, which is the oldest Satavahana inscription, dating back to 100-70 BCE.

**Bedse Caves**

- The Bedse Caves (also known as Bedsa Caves) are a group of Buddhist rock-cut monuments located in the Mavaltaluka of Pune district in Maharashtra, India.
- The history of the caves dates back to the first century BCE during the Satavahana period. They are about 9 km away from the Bhaja Caves. Other nearby caves include the Karla Caves, Patan Buddhist Caves, and Nashik Caves.
- There are two main caves here. The most famous cave is the Chaitya (prayer hall - Cave 7), which has a comparatively large stupa. The second cave is a monastery or vihara (Cave 11). These caves are characterized by decorative niches or chaitya arches.

**Mahakali Caves**

- The Mahakali Caves, also known as the Kondiwita Caves, are a collection of 19 rock-cut Buddhist caves dating from the 1st century BCE to the 6th century CE.

- These Buddhist monasteries are located in the Andheri area of Mumbai (Bombay), Western India.
- The caves are carved out of solid black basalt rock (volcanic trap, with possible erosion).
- The Mahakali Caves consist of 19 rock-cut monuments (4 caves on the southeast face and 15 caves on the northwest face).
- The northwest group of caves dates back to the 4th to 5th century, while the southeast group is older.
- These rock-cut caves have been in existence since the time of the ancient Ashoka Empire, and Buddhist monks used them for habitation and meditation as far back as 2,000 years ago.
- One of the stupas, originally created as a Buddhist monument, is now consecrated as a Hindu lingam statue.
- Inscriptions on the walls are in Pali script.
- The Mahakali Caves are located a few kilometers from Paspoli. According to the inscription, a person from Paspoli donated a vihara to Mahakali.
- From at least the 1st century BCE to the 12th century CE, Mahakali Caves had an active monastery.

**Features**

- The Mahakali Caves are a Buddhist monastery made up of two sets of rock-cut caves. One set has four caves in the northwest, and the other set has fifteen caves in the southeast.
- Most of these caves are viharas and chambers for monks.
- The main cave contains statues of Buddha and stupas, along with Buddha statues carved into the rocks.
- The monument also includes remnants of rock-cut ponds and other structures.
- A unique stupa with a mysterious Buddhist deity statue fell from Cave Number 1 down to the foothill. These statues are now worshiped as Goddess Mahakali in the Juna Mahakali Temple (Old Mahakali Temple).

- The rock here is volcanic basalt, which is not ideal for preservation.
- Only Cave Number 9 is a Chaitya, containing damaged figures of Buddhist myths along with seven Buddha statues.
- The Mahakali Caves have a total of twenty doors, with the southeast caves being older than the northwest caves.
- Some caves also have verandas and courtyards.
- Of the four caves in the northwest group, two were used as residential quarters, while one was used as a dining area.
- Between the two cave groups, several broken stupas/monuments are scattered.
- A simple theater, created for the teacher and students, is one of the more interesting rock-cut monuments. Several broken stone stairs lead from the west to the southern series of caves.
- Cave Number 9, a Chaitya, is a unique cave among the fifteen caves. It is the largest cave of Kondiwita and contains seven depictions of Lord Buddha and other figures from Buddhist mythology.
- Over the centuries, several Buddhist and Shaiva monasteries coexisted in this area. The nearby Jogeshwari Caves are an example of this coexistence.

## Ganeshleni/Leṅyadri/Junnar Caves

- Leṅyadri, also sometimes called Ganesh Lena or Ganesh Hill Caves, is a series of about 30 rock-cut Buddhist caves located about 4.8 kilometers (3.0 miles) north of Junner in Pune district, Maharashtra, India.
- The current name "Leṅyadri" literally means "Cave of the Mountain." It is derived from the Marathi word 'Leṅi,' meaning "cave," and the Sanskrit word 'Adri,' meaning "mountain" or "stone."
- The Leṅyadri caves date between the 1st and 3rd centuries CE and are associated with the Hinayana Buddhist tradition.

- Twenty-six caves are individually numbered. The caves face south and are numbered sequentially from east to west. Caves 6 and 14 are Chaityas (chapels), while the remaining are Viharas (residences for monks).
- Cave 7's two central chambers were originally a Buddhist Vihara, but later they were dedicated to the worship of the Hindu God Ganesh. The remaining cells and halls of Cave 7 have remained in their original form. This Ganesh Lena Vihara is one of the Ashtavinayak temples, a group of eight prominent Ganesh temples in Western Maharashtra. According to local legends, this is the Girijatmaja Cave where Goddess Parvati wished to become a mother and where Ganesh was born.

**Naneghat Caves**

- The Naneghat Pass (Nane means "coin" in Marathi and Ghat means "pass") was one of the trade routes that connected the coastal communities of Konkan to the high plateau of Deccan through Junner.
- They were discovered by William Sykes during a pilgrimage in the summer of 1828.
- This was the most important trade route because it directly connected the ports of Sopara and Kalyan to Junner and Paithan. The name was given because this route was used for toll collection from traders crossing the hills at toll booths. When passing through Malsheswar Ghat, we can easily catch a glimpse of Naneghat after Murbad.
- Inscriptions are attributed to a queen of the Satavahana dynasty. Her name was either Naynika or Naganika, possibly the wife of King Shatakarni.

**Ajanta Caves**

- The Ajanta Caves are Buddhist rock-cut cave monuments located in the Aurangabad district of Maharashtra, dating from the 2nd century BCE to around 480 CE.
- The caves contain paintings and rock-cut sculptures, considered

some of the finest surviving examples of ancient Indian art, particularly the expressive paintings that convey emotions through gestures, posture, and form.

- There are a total of 29 caves, of which 25 were used as viharas (residential caves), and 4 were used as chaityas (prayer halls).
- The caves have 36 identifiable bases, some of which were discovered after the original numbering of caves 1 to 29. The later-discovered caves were assigned alphabetic suffixes, such as 15A, which were identified between the original caves 15 and 16. The numbering of caves follows a tradition of convenience and does not reflect their chronological order of construction.
- The construction of the Ajanta caves occurred in two phases:
  - **Satavahana Period**: The earliest group of caves includes caves 9, 10, 12, 13, and 15A. The murals in these caves depict Jataka tales. The artistic influence of the Gupta period is seen in the later caves, but there are varying opinions on the century in which the earliest caves were created.
  - **Vakataka Period**: The second phase of construction at the Ajanta site began in the 5th century CE. This phase is credited to the Mahayana tradition of Buddhism, often referred to as the "Great Vehicle" tradition. The second phase includes caves 1-8, 11, 14-29, some of which may be extensions of earlier caves. Caves 19, 26, and 29 are chaityas, while the rest are viharas.
- The caves were excavated by Buddhist monks under the patronage of the Vakataka rulers, including Harisena.
- The figures in these caves were painted with frescoes that demonstrate a high level of naturalism. The colours were made from local plants and minerals.
- The outlines of the paintings were drawn in red, and then the inside was painted. The notable absence of the colour blue in the paintings is one of the most remarkable features. Most of the paintings focus on Buddhism, including the life of Buddha and Jataka tales.

- Five caves were constructed during the Hinayana period of Buddhism, while the other 24 were built during the Mahayana period.
- The Ajanta caves are mentioned in the travelogues of Chinese Buddhist pilgrims Fa-hien and Xuanzang.
- Cave 26 features the Mahaparinirvana of Buddha, and Cave 19 features the Naga King and his wife, both of which are among the most famous sculptures in the Ajanta Caves.

**Udayagiri and Khandagiri Caves**

- As the tourist moves ahead from Bhubaneswar, the Udayagiri hills are on the right. Compared to Khandagiri, Udayagiri has more beautiful and well-maintained cave temples. Udayagiri has 18 caves.
- Udayagiri and Khandagiri Caves, formerly known as Kattaka Caves or Cuttack Caves, are partially natural and partially artificial caves of archaeological, historical, and religious significance near Bhubaneswar in Odisha.
- The caves are situated on two adjacent hills, Udayagiri and Khandagiri, which are referred to as Kumari Parvat in the Hathigumpha inscription.
- It is believed that most of these caves were constructed during the reign of King Kharavela for Jain monks as residential blocks.

**Udayagiri Caves**

- Udayagiri means "Sunrise Hill," and it contains 18 caves, while Khandagiri has 15 caves.
- The caves of Udayagiri and Khandagiri, referred to as "Leena" or "Lena" in inscriptions, were mainly excavated during the reign of Kharavela for Jain ascetics' residences.
- The most significant cave in this group is the Rani Gumpha at Udayagiri, which is a two-story monastery. Other important caves include Hathigumpha, Ananta Gumpha, Ganesh Gumpha, Jaya Vijaya Gumpha, Manakapuri Gumpha, Bagha/Bhagha/Bhagra Gumpha, and Sarpa Gumpha.

- The Archaeological Survey of India has listed Udayagiri and Khandagiri caves in the "Must See" list of Indian Heritage.
- At Udayagiri, Hathigumpha (Cave 14) and Ganesh Gumpha (Cave 10) are especially famous for their historically significant sculptures and reliefs. Ranikina Nara (Queen's Palace Cave, Cave 1) is also a large carved cave, intricately adorned with sculptural friezes.
- Khandagiri offers a magnificent view of Bhubaneswar from its summit. The Ananta Cave (Cave 3) displays carvings of women, elephants, athletes, and swans carrying flowers.

## Khandagiri Caves

- When you enter this region from Bhubaneswar, the Khandagiri Hills are on your left. There are 15 caves in Khandagiri, and these caves were renovated during the reign of Uddyotakeshari of the Somavamsi dynasty.
- **Ananta Gumpha:** The cave contains sculptures of women, elephants, swans, etc.
- **Navamuni Gumpha:** The Navamuni Gumpha is a roughly carved chamber containing sculptures of nine Jain Tirthankaras and Sāsanā Devi. These sculptures were added in the 11th century by the Somavansi dynasty.
- **Tusela Gumpha:** Three sculptures of Rishabh Dev in the Kayotsarga posture are found here. In addition to these, there are sculptures of 24 Jain Tirthankaras which appear rough.
- **Ambika Gumpha:** There are three raised sculptures here, two of Rishabh Nath and one of Amra Neminath's Sāsanā Devi.

## Rani Gumpha ("Queen's Cave")

- Among the caves of Udayagiri and Khandagiri, Rani Gumpha is the largest and most popular cave.
- It is a two-story cave, with three wings on each floor, and the central wing is larger than the other two. The lower floor has seven entrances, while the upper floor has nine columns. The upper part of the central wing features sculpted images depicting a king's

victory procession. Several rooms have images of doorkeepers, some of which are distorted.

## Manakapuri and Swargapuri Gumpha

- Manakapuri and Swargapuri Gumpha are two-story caves. In the Manakapuri cave, two male and two female figures are shown worshiping the Kalinga Jin, which Kharavela brought back from Magadha. It contains a damaged Jain religious symbol that was likely used for worship.

- There are three inscriptions: one mentions Kharavela's chief queen, and the other two mention Kharavela's successor, Kudepsiri, and Kudepsiri's son or brother, Badukha.

## Ganesh Gumpha

- The cave is named after the carved image of Ganesh behind its right chamber. It is undoubtedly a later addition and may not be the original sculpture. There are two large statues of elephants wearing garlands at the entrance, and it is the first example of sculptures of deer used as guardians at the cave entrances.

- Additionally, sculpted figures of doorkeepers are found at the entrances. This cave's reliefs narrate the story of the princess of Ujjayini, Basvadatta, escaping with King Udayan of Kaushambi in the company of her lover, Vasantika.

## Vyaghra Gumpha

- Vyaghra Gumpha is one of the most popular caves at Udayagiri. The cave, which is in ruins, has an entrance shaped like a tiger's mouth, with a chamber forming the tiger's throat.

- This cave is one of the most photographed sites in Udayagiri. The word "*Vyaghra*" means "tiger." The inscription found here indicates that the cave belonged to the city judge, Sabhuti.

## Heart of the Cave

- *Hathi Gumpha* is a large natural cave that contains the inscription of Kharavela, which is the main source of information about him. This cave is known as Hathi Gumpha due to its excellent elephant carvings. The word "Hathi" means "elephant" here.

- The Hathi Gumpha Cave (Elephant Cave) contains the Hathi Gumpha inscription, written by King Kharavela of Kalinga during the 2nd century BCE.
- The Hathi Gumpha inscription has seventeen lines carved in deep Brahmi script on the hanging eyebrow of a natural cave on the southern side of the Udayagiri hill. The inscription mentions Kharavela's valor in restoring the position of Agra-Jina (translated as Rishabh Nath), which was taken by the Nanda dynasty. This inscription faces the Ashokan inscriptions at Dhauli, located about six miles away.

## Udayagiri Caves

The Udayagiri Caves are rock-cut caves dating back to the early years of the 5th century CE near Vidisha in Madhya Pradesh. These caves are located on two lower hills on the banks of the Betwa River and its tributary, the Bes River.

- These caves are home to some of India's oldest surviving Hindu and Jain temples and iconography. They are the only site where inscriptions are directly linked to the Gupta period kings.
- The Udayagiri Hills and its caves are one of the most important archaeological sites in India and are preserved and managed as monuments by the Archaeological Survey of India.
- The Udayagiri caves contain Jain statues. They are notable for their ancient monumental relief sculptures of Parshvanatha in his avatar.
- There are important inscriptions from the Gupta dynasty related to Chandragupta II (around 375–415CE) and Kumaragupta I (around 415–55CE).
- The Udayagiri cave complex consists of twenty caves (19 Hindu caves and 1 Jain cave). A prominent feature of this site is the famous Varaha statue, which symbolically represents Earth clinging to the tusks of a boar, as described in Hindu mythology.

## Cave 4: Shaivism and Shaktism

- Cunningham referred to Cave 4 as the "Veena Cave". It presents both Shaiva and Shakti themes.

- The sanctum of the temple is dedicated to Shiva, with a one-faced Linga in the sanctum. Outside the entrance, which is a mandapa now in ruins, there are Matrikas (Mother Goddesses), which have possibly been destroyed due to weathering.

**Cave 5: Vaishnavism**

- Cave 5 is more of a shallow space and includes the famous large Varaha panel of Udayagiri caves.
- It depicts the story of Vishnu's Varaha incarnation rescuing the Earth Goddess in distress. Willis described the relief as the "symbolic centerpiece of Udayagiri."

**Cave 13: Vaishnavism**

- Cave 13 contains a large Anantasayana panel, showing Vishnu resting in the form of Narayana. Below Vishnu's feet are two figures, one a large devotee kneeling in reverence, and a smaller person standing behind him.
- The kneeling figure is commonly interpreted as Chandragupta II, symbolizing his devotion to Vishnu. The other person is possibly his minister, Veersena.

**Tiger Caves**

- The Tiger Caves are a group of monuments carved into nine rocks, located between the southern slopes of the Vindhya mountains in the Dhar district of Madhya Pradesh, central India. These monuments are situated 97 km away from the city of Dhar. The caves are famous for the murals created by ancient Indian artists.
- They were developed around the 6th century CE.
- The best prehistoric artwork can be found in these rock-cut caves. Only five of the original nine caves have survived.
- According to mythology, these caves were constructed by Buddhist monk Datka. The carvings were done between the late 4th century and the early 6th century.
- These caves were first discovered in modern times in 1818.

## Features

- The Tiger Caves, like the Ajanta Caves, were made from rock formations along the banks of a seasonal stream named Baghni.
- Despite their Buddhist origins, only five of the nine caves are still standing.
- All of these caves are rest chambers known as "Vihara," with "Chaitya" or prayer halls usually located at the back.
- Cave 4, also known as Rang Mahal, is the most important of the five remaining caves.
- The Tiger Caves are renowned for their murals. Before the paintings were done, thick brown-orange clay plaster was applied to cover the walls and ceilings.
- A lime primer was applied over the plaster, followed by painting. The use of water-soluble binders mixed with coloured pigments to create permanent, quick-drying artwork is known as the tempera technique.
- The murals depict some of the most refined and sophisticated art, as seen in the Ajanta caves.
- The Ajanta Caves are perhaps the only visible example of Indian murals to the outside world.
- However, it has been established that the tradition which began at Ajanta actually started in ancient times. It did not stop at Ajanta but was carried forward by people of various religions across different parts of India.
- To prepare the surface, a layer of red-brown, coarse, and thick mud plaster was laid on the walls and ceilings.
- When the Bagh Caves were explored, only caves 3 and 4 had survived the ravages of time.
- The paintings at Bagh Caves are examples of the classical Indian art "Golden Age."
- Tempera was used to paint the walls and ceilings of the Viharas, and remnants can still be seen in caves 3 and 4 (and remains caves 2, 5, and 7).

- Cave 2, known as the "Pandav Cave," is the best-preserved cave.
- These artworks are more worldly than spiritual.

**Ellora Caves**

- Ellora (locally known as 'VerulLeni') is located in the Aurangabad district of Maharashtra, India. It is one of the largest rock-cut cave temple complexes in the world, with artifacts dating back from the 6th to the 10th century CE.
- It is a UNESCO World Heritage Site with caves dedicated to Hinduism, Buddhism, and Jainism.

**Features of Ellora Caves**

- In terms of subject and architectural style, the caves represent natural diversity.
- There are 17 Hindu caves (caves 13-29; caves 14 and 15 are famous as Ravana's Ravine and Dashavatara caves, respectively), 12 Buddhist caves (caves 1-12), and 5 Jain caves (caves 30-34, which include Indra Sabha and Jagannath Sabha) reflecting religious harmony prevalent during this period of Indian history.
- Some of the famous caves in Ellora include:
  - The Vishwakarma Cave, also known as the Carpenter's Cave, is a Buddhist Chaitya cave where Buddha is depicted in a teaching pose, with a Bodhi tree behind him.
  - Ravana's Ravine Cave number 14.
  - The Dashavatara Temple, located in Cave number 15.
  - The Kailasa Temple dedicated to Lord Shiva in Cave number 16.
    - It is carved from a single stone and has an open courtyard. It was built under the patronage of the Rashtrakuta emperor Krishna I.
    - A relief showing Ravana shaking the Kailasa mountain can be found on the walls of Kailasa Temple.
    - It is considered one of the greatest sculptures in India.

- The Dhumal Leni Cave 29.
- The Rameshwar Temple is located in Cave 21.
- The Indra Sabha (Cave 32) and Jagannath Sabha (Cave 33) are two famous Jain caves.

## Shivleni Caves

- The Shivleni Caves in Ambajogai, Maharashtra, are rock-cut cave monuments from the time of the Parmar dynasty, specifically from the reign of King Udayaditya (around 1060-1087 CE).
- The caves contain statues of Hindu deities such as Shiva, Sapta Matrikas, and Ganesha.
- The Shivleni Caves are located less than half a kilometer to the northwest of the Yogeshwari Temple, along the banks of the Jaywanti River.
- A local legend claims that the monument was once the wedding hall of the goddess Jogai, which is located near the temple. It is said that the wedding was to be conducted here, but due to supernatural reasons, the elephant and everything inside it turned to stone, which is why it is called the 'Jogai Mandap.'

## Mandapeshwar Caves

- These are also known as Montperir Caves, located near Borivali, Mumbai. They were originally created as Brahmin caves during the Gupta dynasty, but later, they were converted into a Christian cave. Among the ruins of the site, statues of Nataraja, Sada Shiva, and Ardhanarishvara can still be seen.
- Above the cave complex, there is a church and its cemetery.